City of Saints

City of Saints

A Pilgrimage to John Paul II's Kraków

George Weigel

Carrie Gress
Historical Notes

Stephen Weigel
Photographs

IMAGE
New York

Library of Congress Cataloging-in-Publication Data
is available upon request.

ISBN 978-0-553-41890-3
eBook ISBN 978-0-553-41891-0

PRINTED IN THE UNITED STATES OF AMERICA

Book design by Donna Sinisgalli
Maps by Mapping Specialists Ltd.
Cover photographs: (Kraków, Poland) © Getty Images/Christian Kober/John
Warburton-Lee Photography Ltd; (John Paul II) © Getty Images/Pacific Press

3   5   7   9   10   8   6   4   2

First Edition

For the men and women of *Środowisko,*
pioneers of World Youth Day,
with special thanks to Piotr and Teresa

Contents

Down through all generations, the words of Christ echo and resound along with the witness of the Gospel, Christian culture, and the customs that derive from faith, hope, and charity. . . . Can one cast all this off? Can one say no? Can one refuse Christ and all that he has brought into human history?

One time Christ asked the Apostles . . . "Do you too wish to go away?" [John 6:67] Allow the successor of Peter, before all of you gathered here today, to repeat the words of Peter, which constituted his reply to Christ's question: "Lord, to whom shall we go? You have the words of eternal life!" [John 6:68]

—Pope John Paul II, homily on the Kraków Commons,
June 10, 1979

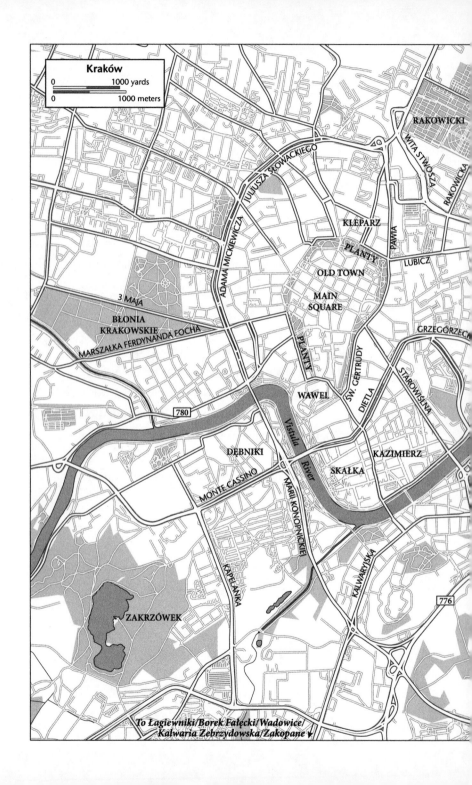

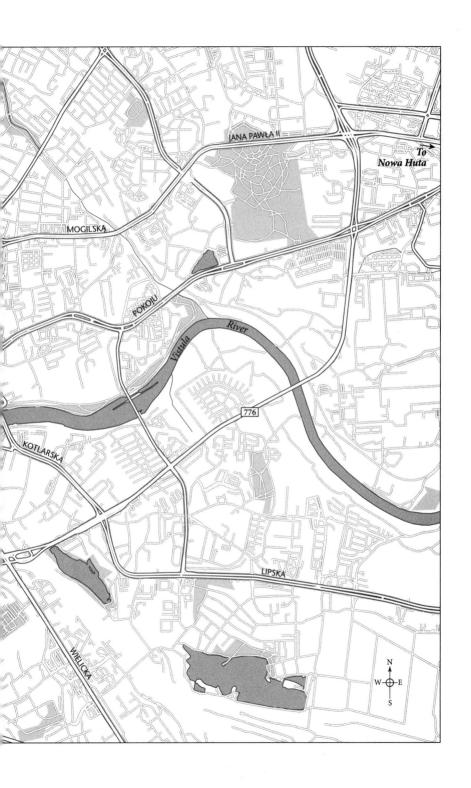

City of Saints

The Main Market Square

Kraków

St. John Paul II and the City Where the Twentieth Century Happened

*W*hen eighteen-year-old Karol Józef Wojtyła, newly arrived in Kraków from provincial Wadowice, walked across the Dębniki Bridge and into Kraków's Old Town in the fall of 1938 to register for his first classes in Polish language and literature at the Jagiellonian University, he may already have felt a sense of kinship with the ancient city that had been Poland's cultural capital for centuries. He had read deeply in his country's poetry, its plays, and its novels; he was a patriot who had begun to grasp the unique role that Poland's culture had played in its singular history; he was a committed Catholic in a city that had given the Church several saints. In moving to Kraków with his widower father, he was, in a sense, moving home.

Still, neither he, his father, those who would be his teachers, nor the men and women who would become his friends imagined that this twenty-minute walk past the site of the martyrdom of St. Stanisław and the great hill of Wawel, with its royal castle and cathedral, was in fact the first moment in a lifelong pilgrimage during which Karol Wojtyła, as Pope John Paul II, would bring a Cracovian sensibility to the world—and in doing *so would bend the curve of history in a more humane direction while leaving an indelible impression on the life and thought of the Catholic Church.*

To follow Karol Wojtyła through Kraków is to follow an itinerary of sanctity while learning the story of a city. Thus, in what follows, the story of Karol Wojtyła, St. John Paul II, and the story of Kraków are interwoven in a chronological pilgrimage through the life of a saint that reveals, at the same time, the richly textured life of a city where a boy grew into a man, a priest, a bishop—and an apostle to the world.

CROSSROAD

Kraków's *Rynek Główny,* the **Main Market Square*** at the heart of the Old City, is the greatest public space in Europe, rivaled only by the Piazza San Marco in Venice for size, architectural achievement, and decorative splendor. To walk through this magnificent example of urban development is to traverse one of the principal crossroads of Europe, in the very heart of Europe. For Poles have never thought of themselves as a part of "eastern Europe"; Poland is in *central* Europe, and the center of Poland, its history and culture, is Kraków.

From the late fourteenth century to the early seventeenth, during more than two hundred years of growth initiated by the marriage of the young Polish queen Jadwiga to the Lithuanian grand duke Władysław Jagiełło, the Polish-Lithuanian

---

*   Sites in **bold** are described in detail in the historical notes.

Commonwealth, with its capital in Kraków, was one of the great powers of Europe. Second only to France in size, it eventually governed a vast expanse of territory reaching from the Baltic in the north to the Black Sea in the south, and from the German *Lander* immediately to the west to the hinterlands of Moscow in the east. Leaving Kraków's **Royal Castle** as the Ottoman Turks closed in on Vienna in 1683, King Jan III Sobieski and the famed Polish heavy cavalry, the Winged Hussars, decisively defeated the last great armed Islamic invasion of Europe. Something of Sobieski's temper, and Poland's, and Kraków's, can be gleaned from the message—a striking variant on Julius Caesar's—sent by the victorious Polish monarch to Pope Innocent XI (along with the green banner of Muhammad, captured from the Ottoman grand vizier): *Veni, vidi, Deus vincit* (I came, I saw, God conquered).

Kraków was far more than the chief city of a great political-military power, however. For the old Polish royal capital was, and is, located on the border between Europe's two wings, the Latin west and the Byzantine east. That location is reflected in the city's striking combination of architectural styles, in which the visitor frequently finds elaborate baroque decoration inside churches crowned with onion domes reminiscent of classic Orthodox church architecture.

Here, in addition to the Latin that was the common tongue of educated people, the local citizens spoke a Slavic language written in the Latin alphabet: another sign that Kraków and Poland were a bridge across traditional cultural divides. Here, during the European wars of religion, a tradition of civility, tolerance, and respect for the rights of conscience was the accepted public norm. There were no religious persecutions in Reformation-era Kraków, no coerced conversions, no burning of heretics. In 1583, Poland's political leaders made a declaration of tolerance, the likes of which could be found nowhere else in Europe: "We who differ in matters of religion will keep the peace among ourselves, and neither shed blood on account of differences of Faith, or kinds of church, nor punish one another by confiscation of goods, deprivation of honor, imprisonment, or exile." Poles and Cracovians were not angels, and intolerance certainly warped individual lives. But the public norm was tolerance; it was embodied in the famous declaration of King Zygmunt II August to the Polish parliament, the Sejm, that "I am not the king of your consciences"; and, as historian Norman Davies once put it, Poland was "a land without bonfires," while much of the rest of Europe self-destructed in the Thirty Years War.

At the height of the Polish-Lithuanian Commonwealth, Kraków was also a major commercial and intellectual metropolis. In the *Rynek Główny,* one could hear a multitude of tongues spoken, buy and sell products from across Europe, plan commercial expeditions to far lands and distant shores. Kraków's economic vitality and the generosity of wealthy Poles helped support one of Europe's greatest centers of scholarship in the middle of the second millennium—a tradition of learning dating back to the Middle Ages, when intellectually adventurous students from this part of the world traveled the long road to Paris to study under Thomas Aquinas. The **Jagiellonian University**, which was once sustained by the philanthropy of Queen Jadwiga, grew out of the Kraków Academy of Theology, and gave Kraków, Poland, the Catholic Church, and the world both saints and men of genius: Jan Kanty, a late medieval biblical scholar canonized in 1767; Mikołaj Kopernik (Copernicus), who changed the world's view of the world's place in the universe; and Paweł Włodkovic, who at the Council of Constance in 1414 inveighed against the Teutonic Knights and their practice of conversion by conquest.

Located above the Vistula River on a rocky promontory at the southern edge of today's Old City, standing watch over Kraków, is **Wawel Hill,** the "Polish Zion." Wawel's Royal Castle and **Cathedral,** a complex of structures woven together over centuries, draws one's gaze upward, evoking the great aspirations that made, and make, Kraków unique. The city ceased to be Poland's political capital in 1596, when King Zygmunt III moved the seat of government to Warsaw. Yet for almost half a millennium, Kraków, no longer a center of political power, has remained the cultural and spiritual capital of Poland. Today, the Polish Zion looks over a thriving city at the very center of Europe.

Wawel Hill

A CITY UNDER PRESSURE

When Poland, the state, was erased from the map of Europe by the Third Polish Partition of 1795—a vivisection conducted by the neighboring great powers of Russia, Prussia, and Austria—Kraków remained one of the great centers of Polish national consciousness. And for a century and a quarter, the years Poles refer to as their national "time on the cross," Kraków's literary, intellectual, and religious life all helped keep alive the idea of "Poland" while the partitioning great powers sought to eliminate that very notion. Tales of past Polish glories were recited or sung, dreams of Polish independence were dreamt, and rebellions were planned in the city's cafes and noble houses. Memories of Poland's greatness were kept alive in the royal crypts of Wawel Cathedral, where generations of Poles under foreign rule could ponder the achievements of Jadwiga and Władysław Jagiełło, Kazimierz the Great and Jan Sobieski. An aesthetic movement, Young Poland, led by men of accomplishment in many artistic fields such as playwright, poet, and painter Stanisław Wyspiański, was centered in Kraków and breathed new life into Polish literature and visual arts. And while the writers, composers, and artists of Young Poland were crafting their distinctive responses to the failure of the Polish rebellion of 1863 to reestablish national independence, so did two men whom the Catholic Church would later recognize as saints: rebels who, having risked their futures in 1863, staked the balance of their lives on a revolution of the spirit in intense forms of consecrated religious life—Rafał Kalinowski and Albert Chmielowski.

These heroic efforts to keep Poland, the nation, alive

during the 123 years that Poland, the state, could not be found on a map seemed vindicated in 1918, when, like a phoenix, the Second Polish Republic arose from the ashes of a Europe that had come to the brink of self-destruction in the Great War, World War I. Politically, the collapse of the Romanov, Hapsburg, and Hohenzollern dynasties in St. Petersburg, Vienna, and Berlin created the conditions for the possibility of Poland recovering its independence. And yes, Poland's new independence was secured in 1920 by the "Miracle on the Vistula," when the forces of Marshal Józef Piłsudski defeated Trotsky's Red Army outside Warsaw and drove it back into Russia. But there would have been no new Polish state to save had Polish culture succumbed to the country's tripartite division and its political extinction. And if the beating heart of Polish culture was to be found in Kraków between 1795 and 1918, then Poland's rebirth in the aftermath of the Great War was made possible, in no small measure, by Kraków.

For a brief period, between the end of World War I and the rise of Hitler and his Nazis, it seemed that Kraków might return to a calmer life as one of the centers of European culture and learning. But it was not to be.

Unlike most other Polish cities during **World War II,** Kraków was spared obliteration by the German blitzkrieg and the Nazi penchant for gratuitous destruction. The Wehrmacht got to Kraków too quickly in September 1939 for the city to become a battleground; as the "capital" of the Nazi slave-state, the *General Gouvernement,* from September 1939 until January 1945, the city's fabric was largely spared; and as the Red Army approached in January 1945, the Germans left too quickly to do too much revenge bombing of historic sites and buildings. But Kraków suffered. And its suffering was beyond the imagining of most westerners.

Schindler's List gave western audiences some sense of what life in occupied Kraków, its ghetto, and **KL-Płaszów,** the local concentration camp, was like. The city of saints and scholars, poets, painters, and dramatists, patriots and tolerant kings was now run by gangsters like Hans Frank, the governor-general of the *General Gouvernement,* and Amon Göth, the psychopathic commandant at KL-Płaszów, located across the Vistula from Kraków's historic Jewish district, **Kazimierz.** These two men, both of whom were executed for war crimes in 1946, embodied Nazi racial contempt for the Poles as Slavic *Untermenschen,* lower life-forms who were to be fed a minimal diet and, over time, worked into extinction, all for the greater glory of the Third Reich.

Frank presided over a vast territory of lawlessness aptly dubbed "Gestapoland" by Norman Davies: in the *General Gouvernement,* there was no rule of law in the ordinary sense of the term, and as a survivor of those draconian five years once put it, "It was not a question of knowing whether you would be alive next Christmas or on your next birthday; it was a question of not knowing whether you would be alive tomorrow morning." Göth, whose theft of Jewish property aroused the ire of the German SS (not for the robbery, but because all such stolen goods belonged to the Third Reich), tortured and murdered prisoners for his amusement.

Even the graphic images of life in occupied Kraków conveyed by Steven Spielberg's film do not convey the full horror of the occupation, which reflected the Nazi contempt for the spiritual and cultural traditions that had made Kraków such a unique place. For, according to the demonic ideology of the Third Reich, the Poles were not just to be ground into the dust physically. Their culture and its religious roots were to be spat upon, trampled down, exterminated. Thus on a fateful, and ultimately fatal, November morning in 1939, more than a hundred professors of the Jagiellonian University were summoned to what was announced as a faculty meeting with German officers in the *Aula* of the university's **Collegium Novum.** The professors were arrested en masse and transported to the Sachsenhausen concentration camp, where many of them died despite widespread international protests

Memorial, KL-Płaszów

at their deportation. The university was shut down, as part of the Nazi effort to decapitate Polish culture; and although the Jagiellonian quickly reconstituted itself as an underground institution, higher learning in Kraków was, formally speaking, over: *Untermenschen* had no need of higher education.

The occupation sought to destroy Kraków's centuries-old and rich Jewish culture, as well as Kraków's Jews, as quickly as possible. The Nazis also had no concern for the long-term survival of the Catholic Church; it was to be tolerated, in a manner of speaking, so long it confined its activities to worship inside its many churches; ultimately, Catholicism would collapse as the Polish people were eliminated. For the short term, however, the vibrant Catholic educational and cultural life that had long characterized Kraków was put under the Nazi ban. Catholic charitable and educational work was forbidden; the Catholic press was shut down; organizing Catholic youth groups was a capital offense. Thus in one example of persecution, the Germans routed out the Salesian priests at the **Church of St. Stanisław Kostka** in the working-class neighborhood of **Dębniki** in May 1941, sending all but one to the Dachau concentration camp, where the Salesians lived in the "priests' barracks" (sometimes described as the world's largest monastery) until they died from exhaustion and illness or were executed.

One-fifth of the prewar population of Poland in September 1939 was dead by the Second World War's end, victims of combat, malnutrition, disease, random murder—and the extermination camps, the greatest of which, **Auschwitz-Birkenau,** pioneered industrialized mass murder thirty-five miles to the west of Kraków, inside that part of the Second Polish Republic that had been absorbed into the German Reich. But any hope that Kraków, and Poland, would be restored to freedom by the defeat of German National Socialism was dashed by the British and American agreement, at the Tehran and Yalta conferences, to give Stalin and the Soviet Union effective control over postwar Poland. World War II, Poles came to say, was "the war we lost twice."

The communist usurpation of Polish liberties was as comprehensive in intent as the Nazi effort to eliminate Poland as a cultural and historical reality. The massacres at Katyn in 1940 cost Kraków dearly, as the NKVD, the Soviet secret police, killed some twenty-three thousand Polish officers, many of them reservists expected to play leading roles in postwar Polish political, cultural, and professional life, who were murdered, one by one, with a bullet in the back of the head. So did the loss of Cracovians who, with the famous Polish II Corps and

"Ecce Homo," Ark Church, Nowa Huta

other formations, had fought with the Allies in North Africa, the Middle East, and France, but who remained in exile after the war's end, unable to return to Poland because of the threat of communist persecution. So did the secret police murders of Poles of impeccable integrity and heroism who had been members of the underground Polish Home Army during the war.

Kraków's tradition of resistance to tyranny remained strong, however, and in the bogus elections of 1946 and 1947, held to provide a veneer of political legitimacy to the Stalinist regime of Bolesław Bierut, the Cracovians returned the highest percentage of anti-communist votes in the country. Payback quickly followed with the communist decision to build a new steel-milling town, **Nowa Huta,** on the outskirts of Kraków— the first town in the thousand-year history of Poland deliberately built without a church. Over the next four decades, the exhaust from Nowa Huta's steel mills would, literally, eat away at the fabric of Kraków, to the point where some of the magnificent facades of the grand old magnate homes facing the Main Square began to crumble. Forty years of communism blackened the Old City, its once vibrant golds, greens, and pastels muted to the point of obliteration by decades of polluted air and the authorities' incompetence and neglect. According to communist theory, "history" is merely the exhaust fumes of impersonal economic processes; in Kraków, the exhaust fumes of Nowa Huta threatened to destroy history, as embodied by the city's distinctive architecture.

As their plans for a churchless Nowa Huta clearly demonstrated, the communist attack on Kraków was spiritual as well as physical. At the height of Polish Stalinism, the Catholic Church was under intense assault throughout Poland:

bishops, priests, and religious brothers and sisters were arrested in their thousands; Catholic charitable institutions were expropriated; the Catholic press was shut down (save for a pseudo-press of pseudo-Catholics); and the communist secret police made every effort to penetrate the Church and suborn its leaders, in an enormous expenditure of public funds that constituted a huge theft from Polish society. Even after the worst depredations of Stalinism ended in the mid-1950s, the Catholic Church in Poland was under constant harassment and pressure, for it embodied the remnant of Polish civil society while continuing its historic role as the safe-deposit box of Polish national identity.

The two great mid-twentieth-century totalitarianisms— German National Socialism and Marxism-Leninism— embodied the worst of the twentieth century. Under Nazism and communism, lethally distorted and murderously false ideas about human nature, human community, and human destiny led to mass slaughter on an unprecedented historical scale. Kraków experienced those horrors in a singular way, and as the communist horror followed hard on the collapse of the Nazi horror, the student of politics may well conclude that Nazism and communism were two variant forms of the same evil political experiment: the complete subordination of the individual to the state.

In Kraków, however, something else happened.

For if Kraków was "the city where the twentieth century happened" in a uniquely sinister way, Kraków was also the city where the answer to the horrors of the twentieth century was given, through a vision of the divine mercy that was carried to the world by a mission-driven man of God.

A MAN AND HIS CITY

Karol Wojtyła came to Kraków in 1938 and stayed precisely forty years: as student, actor, laborer, seminarian, priest, poet, playwright, essayist, sportsman, philosopher, and bishop. Born in 1920 in **Wadowice**, a provincial town some thirty miles to the southwest of the old Polish capital, Wojtyła retained a reverence for his birthplace throughout his life. But it was his adopted city that he habitually referred to as "my beloved Kraków." Seldom, if ever, have a man and a city been better matched. And from that virtually perfect match came historically unexpected things. For Karol Wojtyła took the Cracovian ethos he had begun to assimilate as a student, and the lessons he had learned there as priest and bishop, to the world stage as Pope John Paul II. In doing so, he helped bend the curve of history in a more humane—a more Cracovian— direction.

When Wojtyła was named archbishop of Kraków in December 1963, he was the first of the city's Catholic leaders not to have been a member of the gentry class or the nobility. The man who ordained him a priest, for example, the heroic Adam Stefan Sapieha, was known as the "Prince-Archbishop" because he was the son of a noble Polish-Lithuanian family. Whatever the simplicity of his origins in the lower middle class, however, Karol Wojtyła and Kraków were made for each other—and made for each other, in a Christian perspective, by Divine Providence.

He was a scholar-bishop, with a deep reverence for the life of the mind and a long bibliography of articles and books, in the city that was one of the historic dynamos of Polish intellectual life. He was a man of letters in the center of Polish culture, a writer in the city where the first book in Polish had been published. He was a patriotic Pole in an environment where the history of Poland enveloped him daily, in the very fabric of the city whose Catholic shepherd he had been called to be. He was a radically converted Christian disciple in a city of martyrs, whose witness ran from that of his eleventh-century predecessor as bishop, St. Stanisław (the "Polish Becket") canonized in 1253, to those of his contemporaries murdered "in hatred of the faith" by the Nazis and communists. And he was a man of mystical gifts in a city where an obscure nun, Sister Maria Faustina Kowalska, had died, seven years after having received her first mystical visions of the divine mercy radiating from the sacred heart of the Risen Christ.

In Kraków, Karol Wojtyła learned a heroic concept of the

John Paul II memorial, Skałka

Catholic priesthood and the Catholic episcopacy. As a young member of the clandestine resistance to the Nazi occupation, he witnessed the priests of his parish being deported to Dachau and a slow-motion martyrdom. As an underground seminarian hidden in the bishop's residence, he saw Archbishop Sapieha take the trials of wartime spiritual leadership into his chapel every night, laying his burdens on the Lord, who had told his followers to pick up the cross and follow him. And shortly after the war, he learned of the self-sacrifice of the Franciscan friar Maximilian Kolbe, who had volunteered to take the place of the father of a family in the starvation bunker at Auschwitz, where he died after two weeks of agony.

Ordained an auxiliary bishop of Kraków in 1958 at age thirty-eight, Wojtyła became de facto leader of the archdiocese on the death of Archbishop Eugeniusz Baziak in 1962, when Wojtyła was elected temporary archdiocesan administrator by the cathedral chapter. After a lengthy dispute between Cardinal Stefan Wyszyński and the Polish communist authorities over the succession to Baziak, Wojtyła was finally appointed archbishop and took possession of Wawel Cathedral on March 8, 1964, as the seventy-sixth leader of the Church of Kraków. Over the next fourteen years, he became one of the most dynamic and effective diocesan bishops in the Catholic Church. Then, for the next twenty-six and a half years, he took what he had learned from Kraków to the world, as John Paul II, Bishop of Rome.

Wojtyła's transition from Kraków to Rome was virtually seamless, in that many distinctive characteristics of the pontificate of John Paul II had their origins in his years as archbishop of Kraków. World Youth Day—now a staple feature of global Catholic life—began in Kraków, in Wojtyła's pioneering chaplaincy to university students in the first years of his priesthood. Similarly, John Paul II's magnetism for the young was presaged in the remarkable group of lay friends, known in Polish as *Środowisko*, that first formed around the newly ordained Father Karol Wojtyła when they were university students. His pastoral pilgrimages as pope—during which he flew some 750,000 miles (the equivalent of three trips between the Earth and the Moon)—were foreshadowed in the lengthy parish visitations he made as archbishop of Kraków. His groundbreaking teaching on human sexuality, marriage, and the family reflected his episcopal ministry in Kraków, during which he had founded the Institute for Family Studies as a key component of the archdiocese's ministry—the first institution of its kind in Poland. His steady efforts to provide an authoritative interpretation of the Second Vatican Council in his papal encyclicals, apostolic exhortations, and apostolic letters was a natural outgrowth of the work he had done to implement the Council in Kraków, in a process that was arguably the most comprehensive of any diocese's in the world.

His remarkable command of the world stage—including the nine days of his first Polish pilgrimage in June 1979, during which the history of the twentieth century pivoted and the seeds of the liberation of central and eastern Europe were planted—was possible because of his experience as a public figure in Kraków. For in Kraków, on great religious feasts, Karol Wojtyła, a scholar not given to raising his voice, learned how to be a compelling and commanding public orator, able to summon people of all classes and conditions to a higher vision of their capabilities. And what he often called the "key" to his pontificate, the Great Jubilee of 2000, was deeply influenced by his Polish and Cracovian experience of anniversaries as occasions of spiritual, cultural, and national renewal, especially the celebration of the millennium of Poland's baptism in 1966.

Then there was his Cracovian encounter with Sister Faustina and her visions of the divine mercy.

Karol Wojtyła did not know Sister Faustina, who died in 1938 in the red-brick **Convent of the Sisters of Our Lady of Mercy,** in the Łagiewniki district of Kraków. As it happens, however, that convent is located within a few hundred yards of the chemical plant where the youthful manual laborer who would become pope worked the night shift, carrying large buckets of lime when he was not trying to find a few spare moments to read the philosophical and theological texts he was being assigned in Archbishop Sapieha's clandestine seminary. Clad in denims and wooden clogs, trying to keep warm in the severe Polish winters, young Karol Wojtyła would walk past what had been Sister Faustina's convent almost every day, sometimes stopping to pray in the chapel.

As priest and bishop, Wojtyła was impressed by the impact of the Divine Mercy Chaplet and other aspects of the Divine Mercy devotion that were spreading among his people and throughout Poland, and he came to believe that there was something of global importance in the visions of divine mercy granted Sister Faustina. During the Second Vatican Council, he worked hard in Rome to rehabilitate Sister Faustina's reputation. Thanks in part to a defective Italian translation, her spiritual diary, *Divine Mercy in My Soul,* had been placed on

St. Maria Faustina Kowalska,
Altar of the Three Millennia,
Skałka

the old Index of Forbidden Books (curiously enough, by the pope, John XXIII, who would be canonized with John Paul II on April 27, 2014); Wojtyła asked one of the directors of his second doctoral dissertation, Father Ignacy Różycki, to prepare a critical edition of the diary, which satisfied the Roman authorities about Faustina's orthodoxy and cleared the way for her beatification cause to be introduced.

Wojtyła's work on behalf of Sister Faustina during Vatican II was more than a matter of vindicating a local Cracovian nun whom many regarded as a saint. Karol Wojtyła was a man who deeply believed that there are no coincidences in the mysterious designs and workings-out of Providence. What we experience as "coincidence," he came to understand, is simply a facet of God's saving plans for the world that we do not yet grasp. That understanding led Wojtyła to a profound insight into the modern history of his "beloved Kraków."

If the grotesque brutalities of the lethal twentieth-century totalitarianisms had made Kraków the city in which the worst of the twentieth century had happened, then Kraków was also the city in which the answer to those evils had been given, even as the totalitarian shadows closed in on Poland from the west and from the east. Divine mercy, radiating from the heart of the Risen Christ, was God's answer to the human wickedness that had made the mid-twentieth century a slaughterhouse, the most lethal period in human history.

Karol Wojtyła was a thoroughly modern man who knew the experiences of his times from the inside. He read those experiences, however, not only through the analytic methods of contemporary scholarship but also through lenses ground by biblical faith. And through that distinctively biblical way of seeing and understanding the world, he came, over the course of his life as priest and bishop, to a deep insight into the guilt that tormented the Western world: a guilt that was born of the fact that the West, while imagining itself the center of historical initiative in human affairs, had created two monstrous systems that killed tens of millions of human beings in the middle decades of the twentieth century. Recognized as such or not, articulated in those terms or not, that guilt lay over the late modern world like a pall—a thick, choking fog that impeded visions of a more humane and decent world in the future.

How could twenty-first-century men and women cope with that burden of twentieth-century guilt? To whom could these sins and crimes be confessed? To whom could repentance be offered? From whom could forgiveness be sought? In an apostolic letter on the future of the Catholic Church in a Europe that seemed mired in a guilt from which it suffered but which it could not acknowledge, John Paul II identified this cultural crisis as a profound *spiritual* crisis: "One of the roots of the hopelessness that assails many people today . . . is their inability . . . to allow themselves to be forgiven, an inability often resulting from the isolation of those who, living as if God did not exist, have no one from whom they can seek forgiveness."

But the merciful Father did exist, John Paul knew. The truth about the Father and his infinite mercy had been revealed in the Son's parable of the prodigal son (Luke 15:11-32): God, the divine father who restores to his wayward children the human dignity they often squander, never ceases to forgive those who repent and confess. That truth, announced in the first century by the man his disciples knew as the rabbi Jesus of Nazareth, had been made known once again, almost two millennia later. In one of the darkest periods of human wickedness, God had made the light of the divine mercy shine through the visions of the heart of Jesus Christ, the Risen Lord, given to a self-effacing and humble Polish nun between 1931 and 1938. The culturally stricken and shattered world of the late twentieth and twenty-first centuries, John Paul believed, could find healing in the revelation of divine mercy bestowed on Sister Maria Faustina Kowalska—a healing that, like the Divine Mercy devotion she promoted, was not for Kraków only, but was intended to be taken from Kraków to the whole world.

That was why John Paul II canonized Sister Faustina as the first saint of the Great Jubilee of 2000: because, as he put it at her canonization ceremony, her visions of divine mercy could "illumine the way for the men and women of the third millennium." That is why the Catholic Church now celebrates the Octave of Easter as Divine Mercy Sunday. That is why John Paul II, consecrating the **Basilica of Divine Mercy** in Kraków on August 17, 2002, solemnly entrusted the world to divine mercy, for, as he said in his homily that day, it is "only in the mercy of God [that] the world will find peace and mankind will find happiness!"

Sister Faustina's vision, and John Paul II's mission, brought a Cracovian gift to the entire world.

THE CITY AND THE SOUL OF JOHN PAUL II

There are many ways to "read" Kraków: through a study of its history, its art and architecture, its literary and musical life; through pondering the lives of its saints, some of the most prominent of whom are gathered beneath the Cross of Christ, with Mary and John, in a fine Jubilee 2000 bronze at the rear of the *Rynek Główny*'s **Basilica of the Assumption of Our Lady,** the *Mariacki*. Surely one of the most intriguing ways to learn this extraordinary city is through the Cracovian experience of Karol Wojtyła.

Karol Wojtyła, Pope John Paul II, was a man whose life was the expression of a richly textured and multidimensional soul. The many layers of that soul took on their first mature form in Kraków. They were then developed over the course of Wojtyła's four decades of priestly and episcopal ministry in the city he called home, the earthly abode he loved best. Twenty-six years in Rome obviously shaped the soul of the pope whom the Church would recognize, nine years after his death, as a saint. But it was to Kraków that John Paul II returned, time and again, to find renewed spiritual energy—to find the refreshment for his soul promised by the Lord Jesus to his disciples.

He called it "my beloved Kraków." What he experienced and learned in the city he cherished was that love is stronger than death, for love is the most living thing there is. It was a lesson he took out into a world that had almost destroyed itself by hate—a world that could be healed only by the love whose most powerful and transformative expression is the divine mercy, mediated to the world through Jesus Christ and his Church.

Great Jubilee of 2000 sculpture, Mariacki

Student Pathways

St. Florian, Floriańska Gate

John Paul II Square, Wadowice

Wadowice

Family, Fatherhood, and Fatherland

Preaching at the canonizations of Pope John XXIII and Pope John Paul II on April 27, 2014, Pope Francis called John Paul "the pope of the family." It was an apt description.

No pope in modern history bent greater efforts to lift up the beauty of Christian marriage and to remind Catholic couples and parents of the spiritual dignity that was theirs because of the sacrament they celebrated on their wedding day. No pope more forcefully confronted the sexual revolution's deconstruction of marriage and the family. No pope had ever described married love as an icon of the interior life of the Holy Trinity, as John Paul II did in his *Theology of the Body*. None of his predecessors had given such urgent attention to the culture of life that begins to be nurtured in the family. And while previous popes had described the family as the basic unit of society, John Paul II enriched that concept by describing the family as one of the schools of freedom in which we learn the habits of mind and heart essential to sustaining democracy and the free economy.

The roots of John Paul's witness to marriage and the family, and the roots of his teaching about the beauty of human love, can be found in Wadowice.

The drama of young Karol Wojtyła's family life left an enduring imprint on his personality and his priesthood. An older sister, his parents' second child, had died shortly after birth. His mother died before the son she called "Lolek" turned nine. When Lolek was twelve, his older brother, Edmund, a physician, died of the scarlet fever he had contracted from a patient for whom he was caring. Under those circumstances, young Karol Wojtyła might have remembered Wadowice primarily as a town of sorrows. By the light of the faith that grew in him there, Wadowice became something quite different: it became the town where the boy who would become one of the most consequential figures of his time, and a saint, learned his first lessons in fatherhood, religious tolerance, patriotism, and the transformative power of suffering borne in faith and hope.

THE CENTRAL FIGURE in the life of young Karol Wojtyła was his father, also named Karol, a retired army officer whom everyone in Wadowice called "the Captain."

He was a man of granite-like integrity who bore his great losses—the death of a daughter, a wife, and a son—with the strength offered by faith. Night after night, Lolek saw his father on his knees in prayer in the **Wojtyła family home,** across the street from the **Church of the Presentation of the Blessed Virgin Mary,** where they worshipped. Shortly after his wife's death, Karol Wojtyła Sr. took his son to see the outdoor passion play at nearby **Kalwaria Zebrzydowska,** a Holy Land shrine built by a local nobleman in the seventeenth century.

That pilgrimage is sometimes remembered for the (perhaps apocryphal) story of the moment when the nine-year-old future pope, having wandered into the tent where the actors were relaxing after the first day of the play, was shocked to see "Jesus" drinking a beer. More important, the experience of the Kalwaria passion play helped teach Lolek the lesson his father had likely intended in taking him there, while they were still in mourning for a wife and mother: our lives are best understood, and our sorrows are best borne, when they are recognized as "playing" within a drama that God himself entered, in the person of his Son, so that the human drama might become, through the redemption, a divine comedy, not a cosmic tragedy or absurdity.

The Captain's example of quiet, steady faith nurtured in constant prayer taught the young boy that manliness and prayerfulness are not antinomies; manliness is expressed by going down on one's knees in worship of the God who comes into human history as a liberator. His father's example and teaching also planted in his son the idea, which he would later develop as a priest and bishop, that all Christian living begins with radical conversion to Christ. The institutional church exists to foster conversion, to offer the possibility of friendship with Jesus Christ. The Church we see, in other words, is in service to a mystery we cannot see but which we can nevertheless experience: the mystery of God's grace, at work in us sacramentally; the mystery of the Kingdom of God breaking into history, *now*.

Some six decades later, reflecting on his father's influence on his life and vocation in *Gift and Mystery*, a memoir written for the golden jubilee of his priestly ordination, John Paul II said that the example of his father had been a kind of "first seminary" for him. For a man still in awe of the gift of the priesthood that he had been given, no finer filial tribute from son to father could be imagined.

WADOWICE, IN KAROL Wojtyła's youth, had a population of some ten thousand souls, one-fifth of whom were Jews. The town was not without prejudiced people, but the public tone was one of tolerance, encouraged by both the local military garrison and by the local priests. In Wadowice, Christian Poles and Jewish Poles thought of each other as fellow citizens. Here, priests such as Father Leonard Prochownik and Father Edward Zacher preached respect for the religious convictions of all and embodied the conviction of Poland's great national poet, Adam Mickiewicz, that Jews were Christians' "elder brothers" in the faith of Abraham and the worship of the one, true God. Here, young Karol Wojtyła began to develop that sensitivity to the drama and agony of twentieth-century Jewry that would be the foundation on which he recast Jewish-Christian relations for the twenty-first century.

The father of his closest Jewish friend and classmate, Jerzy Kluger, had been an officer in the Polish Legion of Marshal Józef Piłsudski, which had been instrumental in reestablishing Poland's independence in 1918. The elder Karol Wojtyła gave private lessons in Polish history to Lolek and his friend Jurek Kluger, illustrating the themes he was developing by reference to poets such as Cyprian Kamil Norwid, one of those brilliant writers who kept the idea of "Poland" alive during the century and a quarter when Poland was partitioned among

Apartment interior, the Family Home of John Paul II Museum

the neighboring great powers. At a moment in Polish history when there was considerable political division between those who imagined "Poland for Poles" and those who were comfortable with the idea (and reality) of a Poland in which Poles, Jews, ethnic Germans, ethnic Ukrainians, and others lived in harmony, the Captain was firmly in the latter camp. His Polish patriotism never veered into xenophobia or racial nationalism.

It was a lesson Lolek learned well. As John Paul II understood these things, national identity and patriotism, rightly understood, ought to lead to a respect for the national identities and patriotic convictions of others. One began to grasp universal truths—like the moral imperative of respect for basic human rights—not from generalized abstractions but from particular experiences. Men and women of different religious and ethnic backgrounds could come to common understandings of the truths on which decent societies rested. It took work. But the work paid off in a public spirit of civility and mutual respect. That was the experience of Wadowice— and a lesson the town's most famous son would try to teach an entire world.

AS A BRILLIANT schoolboy in Wadowice's fine public schools, Karol Wojtyła excelled in virtually every subject. But his greatest interests were in language, literature, and the theater— interests first planted and nurtured in Wadowice that would remain with him throughout his life. Looking back on his schoolboy days, John Paul II wrote, perhaps just a little sheepishly, that he had been "completely absorbed by a passion for literature, especially dramatic literature, and for the theater." From that theatrical passion and experience grew a specific set of skills that he would deploy to great effect on the stage of world history—a sonorous, compelling voice; a remarkable sense of timing in his speech—and a special way of looking at the world, and at words.

While nineteenth-century European Romantic literature was replete with revolutionary fervor, often of a violent sort, Polish Romanticism was different. Novelists, poets, playwrights, and pamphleteers inspired by the French Revolution thought of "revolution" as a comprehensive rejection of the past; the literary men of Polish Romanticism thought of "revolution" as the recovery of something lost, something that had been essential to the formation of "Poland." Thus while other European Romantics rejected Christianity root and branch, Polish Romanticism embraced Christianity as one of the essential seeds from which the unique reality of "Poland" had grown. And that past suggested possibilities for the future: a revolution of the spirit, shaped by the truths of Christian doctrine and Christian morality, could change the course of events, frustrating the designs of tyrants.

In Wadowice, young Karol Wojtyła learned from the national poet Adam Mickiewicz that history has a deep spiritual dimension, and that national suffering can be the prelude to national liberation, if that suffering is borne in faith. It was in Wadowice that Lolek first read the playwright Juliusz Słowacki, a mystic who wrote of a "Slav Pope" who would be a "brother" to all humanity. In Wadowice, young Wojtyła also read deeply in the works of the nineteenth-century poet Norwid, who taught that "a man is born on this planet to give witness to the truth" (a conscious echo of Christ's reply to Pontius Pilate), and that Christ and the Gospel had led humanity from fatalism to freedom—a sharp contrast to the "atheistic humanism" being propagated throughout Europe by thinkers such as Comte, Feuerbach, Marx, and Nietzsche, who insisted that the God of the Bible had to be jettisoned in the name of human maturation and liberation.

And it was in Wadowice that Lolek met, and came under the influence, of Mieczysław Kotlarczyk and his idea of a "theater of the inner word." As both a Christian and a man of the drama, Kotlarczyk believed that theater was an arena of truth-telling in which the spoken word could convey deep truths, if it was spoken freely and clearly enough. Thus he pioneered an avant-garde form of drama in which, stripped of props and costumes, the actor's function was not unlike that of a preacher: breaking open "the word" so that its power to transform lives could be unleashed. In Kotlarczyk's notion of theater, the actors minimized themselves in service to the words they spoke and the truths those words unveiled. Throughout the future pope's high school years, Kotlarczyk drilled the young Karol Wojtyła in how to articulate, with precision, a poem or a line of dialogue so that the power of the truth it contained exploded in the consciousness of the audience.

HIS FATHER'S TUTORIALS, his immersion in Polish literature, and his theatrical work with Mieczysław Kotlarczyk were all crucial in developing the Polish dimension of Karol Wojtyła's multifaceted soul.

John Paul II's Polish soul was formed by his country's singular experience of death and resurrection, which in turn gave him a distinctive view of history and its unfolding. For 123 years, the Polish nation survived the destruction of the Polish state—and survived with such vigor that it could give birth to a new Poland that, after the draconian trials of World War II and communism, would help give the entire West a new birth of freedom. How did that happen? Poland the nation survived the demolition of Poland the state through its culture: its language, its literature, and its Catholic faith. Young Karol Wojtyła learned that crucial fact of his country's history as a young man in Wadowice, from his father and his other mentors. And from that particular fact about the history of Poland, the mature Karol Wojtyła, as priest, bishop, and pope, derived a universal lesson: the most dynamic force in history is neither politics nor economics, but culture.

"History" is not the quest for power, understood as my ability to impose my will on you, as the bloody-minded Jacobins of the French Revolution and their followers claimed. Nor is "history" the exhaust fumes of economics, as the Marxists and their followers taught. *Culture* is what drives history over the long haul. And at the heart of culture, as at the beginning of the word "culture," is cult, religion: what men and women believe, cherish, and worship; what men and women are willing to stake their lives, and their children's lives, on. Secular modernity, in either its Jacobin or Marxist form, may deem religion a historical and political irrelevance. The history of Poland, however, refuted that secular cynicism. Biblical faith, at the center of a rich culture, could be a force for human liberation. The powerless may have seemed defenseless, as those who wielded worldly power measured such things. But the powerless could wield a unique form of power: the power of conviction, shaped by culture, which is a power stronger than death.

The Jacobin myth (that politics controls history) and the Marxist myth (that economics drives history) had helped make a slaughterhouse of the twentieth century. Having learned an alternative view of history in the Wadowice of his youth, John Paul II never succumbed, as a man, to the tyranny of the possible. Where others looked at history and saw only obstacles and intractable situations, he saw possibilities. Believing that the human spirit and its built-in yearning for truth and goodness had not been extinguished in the modern world, he could summon men and women to dream dreams of liberation, and then fulfill them, by deploying the power of the powerless, which is the power of living in the truth—the truth about the dignity of every human person.

———

KAROL WOJTYŁA RECEIVED the sacrament of Confirmation on May 3, 1938. Sometime afterward the archbishop of Kraków, Adam Stefan Sapieha, visited Wadowice and its Marcin Wadowita Secondary School. As the school's most distinguished student, young Karol Wojtyła was chosen to give a welcoming address to the archbishop. Sapieha was impressed and asked Father Edward Zacher, the local pastor, whether he thought they could make a priest out of this young man. Father Zacher said that that didn't seem possible; Wojtyła had been admitted to the **Jagiellonian University** in Kraków, where he intended to study language and literature while continuing his interest in the theater. "A pity," the archbishop was said to have replied.

The star student and the aristocratic archbishop would meet again, under circumstances that neither one of them could have imagined at that meeting in the spring of 1938. But Sapieha was not mistaken in sensing in Karol Wojtyła the beginnings of a priestly vocation. Those seeds had been planted by the example of his father and nurtured by the riches of Polish culture and Catholic piety that flowed, like the Skawa River, through Wadowice and its environs. In this provincial town, Wojtyła experienced the vibrancy of Catholic faith as a culture-forming and history-shaping life commitment: friendship with Jesus Christ did not lead to withdrawal inside the shell of the autonomous self but into an enriched encounter with others and with the world. In Wadowice, the notion of the Catholic priesthood as a form of spiritual paternity began

Basilica of the Presentation of the Blessed Virgin Mary

to take root in his soul. And in Wadowice, the young man who would bend the course of world history in a more humane direction forty years later first learned that such things were possible, in the power of faith and moral conviction.

Wadowice

The first permanent settlements in this area of the Silesian foothills date to the tenth or eleventh century. Wadowice was established in 1327 and for centuries was an average and rather unremarkable Polish village.

The third and final partition of Poland in 1795 led to a period of growth in Wadowice, thanks to a major road that was built through this part of Austrian Galicia, connecting the Hapsburg capital, Vienna, to Lwów (or Lemberg, as it was known in German). As the midpoint along this road between the two cites, Wadowice became a provincial administrative center within the Austro-Hungarian Empire, a position that brought with it trade and commerce, education and culture. While never large, Wadowice did not lack cultural amenities; it was a small town in which the arts and theater flourished.

The Holocaust of European Jewry destroyed a tradition of tolerance and civility in Wadowice, where for centuries Jews and Catholics had lived together harmoniously. During World War II, the entire Jewish population of Wadowice, some two thousand souls, was destroyed, either by immediate execution or by deportation to Auschwitz after the Jewish ghetto was liquidated in August 1943. (The ghetto was itself a result of Wadowice's incorporation into the Third Reich, after Nazi Germany and Soviet Russia divided the remains of conquered Poland in 1939 and the Germans renamed the town Wadowitz.)

Wadowice remained a local administrative center during the communist period of Poland's history, when it was home to several industries that collapsed because of economic inefficiency after the Revolution of 1989.

The election of its native son, Karol Wojtyła, to the papacy in October 1978 had a dramatic effect on Wadowice, which suddenly came to the attention of the international media. Over the twenty-six and a half years of John Paul II's papacy, and in the years after his death, Wadowice has become a major tourist center, receiving pilgrims from all over the world. With a twenty-first-century population of some twenty thousand, Wadowice hosts two hundred thousand visitors annually.

The Family Home of John Paul II
ul. Kościelna, 7

The future pope was born on May 18, 1920, in a small apartment across the street from the local parish church. Here, at Kościelna (Church) 7, young Karol Wojtyła lived with his parents, Karol senior and Emilia, and his brother, Edmund, until his mother died on April 13, 1929, a few weeks before her younger son made his first holy communion. Edmund Wojtyła, born in 1906, and thus fourteen years older than his brother, left home when Karol was a young boy to pursue medical studies in Kraków, where he was awarded his degree in 1930. He died in 1932 in the nearby town of Bielsko after contracting scarlet fever from one of the patients for whom he was caring in the local hospital.

The Wojtyła apartment, which is now the centerpiece of a fine museum completed in 2014, consisted of two rooms and a kitchen on the second floor of a substantial building just across from the parish church. From its windows, the Wojtyła family could see the motto inscribed above the sundial on the church's south wall: CZAS UCIEKA WIECZNOŚĆ CZEKA (Time flies, eternity awaits).

The family-apartment portion of the museum includes many of the Wojtyła family's personal possessions, including an oven, a shelf, a table and tableware, a laundry basket, and family pictures. Other galleries introduce the visitor to Wadowice's Jewish population, the life of the town while the future pope was growing up there, and Wojtyła's activities as a skier, kayaker, and hiker. Artifacts from the papacy of John Paul II include the Browning semiautomatic that Mehmet Ali Agca used to shoot the Pope on May 13, 1981. A display of John Paul's encyclicals is presented in tasteful iconography. The Bible that was read to John Paul II on his deathbed is displayed, as is the Book of the Gospels that rested on his coffin in St. Peter's Square on April 8, 2005.

The Basilica of the Presentation
of the Blessed Virgin Mary
Main Square (John Paul II Square)

The baroque church of the Presentation of the Blessed Virgin Mary is situated at one end of the Wadowice town square. St. Mary's, as the church is called locally, was the center of young Karol Wojtyła's sacramental life. Here he received the three sacraments of initiation: baptized in 1920, he received his first holy communion here in 1929 and was confirmed here in 1938. Here, Wojtyła prayed daily, received the sacrament of penance, served Mass as an altar boy, and became part of a Marian sodality, receiving the brown scapular he would wear throughout his life. Here, in prayer before the image of Our Lady of Perpetual Help, he took his first steps in the Marian piety that, in a refined form, would be a centerpiece of his spiritual life for decades. Here he participated in the rituals of popular piety— processions on great feast days, the veneration of the saints, private and communal recitation of the rosary—to which he remained devoted, and in which he discerned great spiritual power.

The first church in Wadowice, a small wooden structure, was built in the fourteenth century. In the fifteenth century, the

CZAS UCIEKA WIECZNOŚĆ CZEKA

Sundial, Basilica of the Presentation of the Blessed Virgin Mary

townspeople erected a new brick church, which included the Gothic chancel that remains today. After a fire in 1726 destroyed much of the church, St. Mary's was rebuilt in a late baroque style and consecrated in 1808. Two side chapels, flanking the sanctuary, were added shortly after: the Chapel of Christ Crucified, to the right of the sanctuary, and the Chapel of St. Anne, also known as the Holy Family Chapel, to the left. Karol Wojtyła was baptized in the latter on June 20, 1920, and here he venerated the baptismal font on his first papal pilgrimage to Poland, in June 1979. A new facade and clock tower were added to the church in 1896.

In 1992, St. Mary's was elevated to the rank of minor ba-

Baptismal font, Basilica
of the Presentation of the
Blessed Virgin Mary

silica by John Paul II. In 2000, the church was renovated and redecorated in anticipation of its most famous parishioner's silver jubilee as Bishop of Rome. The redecorated interior features polychrome frescoes based on nine of John Paul II's encyclicals, with other motifs drawn from biblical scenes. The Chapel of the Holy Cross in the rear of the basilica houses a miraculous picture of Our Lady of Perpetual Help, crowned by John Paul II on June 16, 1999, during his third papal visit to his hometown. The crown was cast from melted wedding rings and other jewelry provided by the people of Wadowice, who offered this gift to the Virgin Mary through the hands of their townsman.

John Paul II Square

Wadowice's main square was officially renamed for the town's most famous son during his pontificate. Like its counterparts throughout Poland, the square in Wadowice includes shops, restaurants, administrative buildings, and the parish church. Here, too, is the elementary school that young Karol Wojtyła attended, developing friendships that would last a lifetime. From 1926 to 1930, Wojtyła attended the General School for Boys, now a government building on the square, a few hundred feet from St. Mary's. From 1930 to 1938, he went to the Marcin Wadowita Secondary School at Mickiewicza 16; built in 1866, the school still serves as Wadowice's grammar school. A plaque mounted at the school's entrance commemorates Wojtyła's years as a student.

The square is also the site of the Wadowice Municipal Museum, at Kościelna 4, opposite John Paul II's family home. The building was once home to a creamery and restaurant, where the elder Karol Wojtyła and his son would frequently take their meals after Emilia Wojtyła's death in 1929. A tourist information

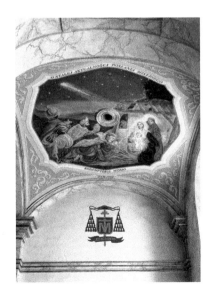

Redemptoris Missio *fresco,*
Basilica of the Presentation of
the Blessed Virgin Mary

office is on the ground floor today, while the Municipal Museum is found upstairs.

On April 8, 2005, the day of Pope John Paul's funeral, thirty thousand people from Wadowice and the surrounding area took part in a Mass in John Paul II Square. The date and hour of his death have been permanently recorded on the old sundial on the south wall of St. Mary's.

A second church, St. Peter's, was erected in Wadowice in 1985 as a *votum* offering, in thanksgiving for Karol Wojtyła's election to the papacy and his surviving the assassination attempt of May 13, 1981.

Kremowki, the cream-filled pastries made famous by John Paul II's fondness for them, are available throughout the town. [C.G.]

Dębniki

The Mystery of Vocation

When eighteen-year-old Karol Wojtyła moved into a small flat at **Tyniecka 10** in Kraków's **Dębniki** neighborhood, he imagined for himself a future rather different than others imagined for him.

In that summer of 1938, as he prepared for his first year

St. Stanisław Kostka Church

of studies at the **Jagiellonian University**, he imagined living out his Christian vocation as a layman: a man of the theater, an actor and director; later, perhaps, a professor of Polish language and literature. Many of his friends, by contrast, thought that he was destined for the Catholic priesthood. In *Gift and Mystery*, written more than five and a half decades after his freshman year of university, John Paul II remembered having resisted these suggestions of a priestly vocation, not because he thought poorly of the Catholic priesthood—those who knew him in Wadowice believed that one of the younger local priests, Father Kazimierz Figlewicz, was something of a hero to Lolek when he was a boy—but because he thought God had other things in mind for him.

"Vocation," as the Catholic Church understands the term, is not the same as "career." The word comes from the Latin verb *vocare*, "to call." And as young Karol Wojtyła came to understand during his years in Dębniki, that etymology contains a deep spiritual truth. Vocation is not so much a matter of choosing as a matter of being chosen, of being called, and that can apply to an extraordinarily wide variety of options. The Catholic Church believes that God in his providence has something unique in mind for every human being, because every man and woman is a unique spark struck from the fiery Godhead of Father, Son, and Holy Spirit. Or to put it differently, God has a unique vocation in mind for every Christian: a certain something that is unique to that individual person.

"Being called," then, is not something that happens only to those in Holy Orders or consecrated religious life, like monks, friars, and religious sisters who take solemn vows of poverty, chastity, and obedience. God has a vocation in mind for *everyone*. And as the biographies of the saints show, many men and women whom the Church later recognized as having lived lives of heroic virtue fought back, resisted the call, denied it—even ran away from it.

Vocational discernment, then, is no simple business. Listening rarely is. During his years in Dębniki, under quite extraordinary circumstances, Karol Wojtyła—the young actor who had spent innumerable hours learning to be a disciplined speaker—learned how to be a disciplined and attentive listener. Listening to God's call amidst the cacophony of a world war in which his country was conquered and then occupied made that learning even more dramatic than it otherwise might have been. Since the days of the catacombs, future popes have not normally discerned their priestly vocations amidst lethal persecution, including the daily threat of random death at the hands of the wicked and the brutal.

Yet that is what Karol Wojtyła learned in the six years he lived in Dębniki. He learned how to listen to what the God he worshipped was asking him to do next. And he learned how to conform his will to the divine will, confident that the divine mercy would sustain him.

THE HOUSE AT Tyniecka 10 into which Karol Wojtyła moved with his father in the summer of 1938 was originally built by Lolek's uncle, his mother's brother, on the south side of the Vistula River. Emilia Wojtyła's two surviving sisters lived on the top two floors. Karol Wojtyła Sr. and his son moved into a basement flat with a corridor separating two sets of rooms: bedrooms for the two men to the left, a kitchen and bathroom to the right. The house's location offered a fine view of Kraków's Old Town and it was only a twenty-minute walk to the Jagiellonian, but the flat had little else to commend it. Because it was dark and sometimes damp, Lolek's friends took to calling it "the catacombs," and in the bitter Polish winters it was hard to keep the chill out with an old-fashioned coal-fired tile stove. Creature comforts were never high on Karol Wojtyła's personal priority list, however, and the vast energy with which he threw himself into his studies at the Jagiellonian and into the university's theatrical circles left him little time to worry about his accommodations, even if he had been inclined to do so.

And then war came.

On the morning of September 1, 1939, Karol Wojtyła had walked across the Dębniki Bridge and up Wawel Hill to serve

Tyniecka 10, exterior

the early morning Mass for his mentor from Wadowice, Father Figlewicz, who had been reassigned to the cathedral. As Luftwaffe bombs began to fall on the city, Father Figlewicz quickly concluded the Mass and Lolek ran back across the bridge to see if his aging father was all right. Like many others, they decided to head east, out of the path of Hitler's Wehrmacht and its blitzkrieg. But after two weeks, still homeless and now part of a great migration of refugees, they found themselves confronted by another totalitarian war machine, Stalin's Red Army, advancing into Poland from the east. So father and son retraced their steps back to Kraków and the Dębniki apartment.

There, young Karol Wojtyła began to confront in earnest the mystery of suffering, about which he would write an extraordinary apostolic letter, *Salvifici Doloris* (Redemptive Suffering), forty-five years later.

Tyniecka 10, Wojtyła apartment

In one of the most challenging passages in the New Testament, Paul writes to his fractious Corinthian converts in these striking terms: "For the sake of Christ, then, I am content with weaknesses, insults, hardships, persecutions, and calamities; for when I am weak, then I am strong" (2 Corinthians 12:10). Years before he began to explain this text in his preaching, Karol Wojtyła gained an insight into St. Paul's seemingly counterintuitive claims about contentment with suffering and about weakness as strength. As had so often been the case before in his young life, his father was his spiritual guide.

The Captain, Karol Wojtyła Sr., was not in robust health when he and his son moved to Dębniki from **Wadowice**. Under the depredations of the German occupation, he grew weaker and weaker, even as his son, compelled to work in a quarry and then a chemical factory to avoid being deported to the Third Reich as slave labor, scrounged for food to sustain the two of them. Yet there were, it seems, no complaints. Karol Wojtyła Sr. may have had little theological training beyond the catechism. Yet he lived the truth of what Paul told the Corinthians the Lord Jesus had said to him: "My grace is sufficient for you" (2 Corinthians 12:9). The father's patience in suffering, and the strength of faith he displayed in his weakness, made a powerful and lasting impression on the son—who, in his turn, would teach the world a lesson about suffering borne in faith when his own time came.

The "seminary" that was his father's example closed, in the house at Tyniecka 10 where it had been located since the summer of 1938, on February 18, 1941. There, alone during the day while his son was out breaking rocks in the **Zakrzówek** quarry, Captain Karol Wojtyła died. The son, discovering that his last immediate relative had died when he returned home that night, wept at his father's bedside, summoned the local priests to give his father the last rites, and later told a friend, "I never felt so alone."

Yet the desolate desert, literally and metaphorically, is often a place of Christian learning. And in young Karol Wojtyła's loneliness, the divine call to a life of priestly self-sacrifice began to be heard a bit more clearly.

OTHER MENTORS HELPED focus Karol Wojtyła's vocational discernment in the Dębniki years. One of them was the man the future pope would later call an unexpected apostle: Jan Tyranowski, the man who would begin to shape the Carmelite and Marian dimensions of St. John Paul II's multilayered soul. Tyranowski was thirty-nine years old when Karol Wojtyła first met him in 1940. He had finished elementary school and a business course that qualified him as an accountant. But bookkeeping was not to his liking, so he took up work in his family's tailoring business. Dapper and shy, he found his life changed one day when he heard a sermon at the Dębniki parish church, St. Stanisław Kostka, in which the homilist insisted that "it's not difficult to be a saint." The idea seized Tyranowski's imagination. He made a vow of celibacy and began to study the classics of Carmelite mysticism. Those works led him, in turn, to a daily practice of prayer and meditation more rigorous than that being lived in many local convents and monasteries—spiritual exercises that he recorded in diaries he kept in his fine, almost calligraphic hand.

Jan Tyranowski could seem, at first blush, somewhat stiff. Yet those who took the trouble to get to know him soon learned that he had the ability to make the Catholic doctrines he taught the young seem like living realities, not abstractions— and he did so by making it clear to his young charges that these truths were something of which he had a daily experience. Thus Tyranowski embodied the ancient Christian tradition that prayer and contemplation—meditating on the truths of the Gospel in a spirit of prayer—are a way of entering into the presence of God, of resting in the Lord, and of being nourished by God's grace. (An hour and a half away, while

Jan Tyranowski shrine, St. Stanisław Kostka Church

Tyranowski was teaching the young men of Dębniki how to pray, Father Maximilian Kolbe demonstrated the practice of the presence of God in an extraordinary way: in his ministry to those condemned to die with him in the starvation bunker at the Auschwitz concentration camp.)

Tyranowski and young Wojtyła likely met at one of the parish's Saturday evening programs for young people, but it was the war that brought them into close—and, for Wojtyła, decisive—contact. On May 25, 1941, the Gestapo raided the Salesian rectory at St. Stanisław Kostka and deported most of the priests to the Dachau concentration camp, where many of them died. The remaining priest asked Tyranowski, at the risk of his life, to take charge of the parish's ministry to young men. The reclusive, mystically inclined tailor took up the challenge and began to organize the parish's young men into what he called "Living Rosary" groups—fifteen men (for the complete mysteries of the rosary as it was then prayed) led by a particularly mature young man, who was known as an "animator." Karol Wojtyła was one of the first animators of Tyranowski's Living Rosary, and the impact on his life would be permanent.

Tyranowski spent extra time instructing and forming the animators of the Living Rosary, and as he got to know Karol Wojtyła better, it must have seemed to him that this already prayerful young man, who had been writing poems and plays since he was in high school, would appreciate the writings of the poet, mystic, and reformer of the Carmelites, St. John of the Cross, whose work Tyranowski knew well. So the tailor of Dębniki began to feed Lolek the works of the Spanish saint, in which the Cross, rather than an absurdity, is the center of the

*Chapel of the Salesian martyrs of World War II, St. Stanisław
Kostka Church*

spiritual life and the ultimate warrant of God's love for humanity. Karol Wojtyła would later write a doctoral dissertation in theology, *Faith According to St. John of the Cross,* but the deeper Carmelite imprint on his spiritual life came from Tyranowski. Under his tutelage, Wojtyła learned that the "shape" of the Christian life is cruciform: that the life of faith involves conforming oneself to the will of the Father, confident, like the Son, that the Father will vindicate those who follow the Father's will, even into the extremity of death. Through Jan Tyranowski, Karol Wojtyła began the lifelong journey toward an understanding of St. Paul's boast that what seemed like folly to some and nonsense to others was the truth by which the world is saved: the truth of "Jesus Christ, and him crucified" (1 Corinthians 2:2).

Jan Tyranowski left another indelible imprint on young Karol Wojtyła's soul and spiritual life, offering him a mature way to live the Marian devotion that was so central to Polish popular piety. In *Gift and Mystery*, John Paul II wrote that when he left Wadowice for Kraków in 1938, the conventional Marian piety of his hometown seemed to him a distraction from focusing his spiritual life on deepening his friendship with Jesus Christ. He may have mentioned this to Tyranowski; in any event, it was Tyranowski who introduced Wojtyła to the works of St. Louis Grignion de Montfort, a French theologian who lived in the late seventeenth and early eighteenth century. Despite the florid style in which he wrote, Montfort had a clear idea of the place of "true devotion to Mary" (as he titled his masterwork) in the Christian scheme of things. All such true devotion, Montfort proposed, was both Christocentric and Trinitarian. As at the wedding in Cana—"Do whatever *he* tells you" (John 2:5)—Mary's role in salvation history, and in the Church, is always to point us toward her son. And because her son is Son of God as well as son of Mary, the Blessed Mother constantly and faithfully points those who follow her toward the two central mysteries of Christian faith: the Incarnation (God has become man) and the Trinity (God is three divine Persons).

Montfort, mediated to Karol Wojtyła through Jan Tyranowski, would thus help hone a Marian theology and piety that John Paul II would offer the entire world Church, teaching that Mary is the first of disciples, in whose conformity to the divine will we find the pattern of all authentic discipleship. Mary is thus also Mother of the Church, as Pope Paul VI entitled her in 1964; and it would be the young man whom Jan Tyranowski introduced to the theology of Louis Grignion de

Montfort who would have a mosaic of Mary, *Mater Ecclesiae,* mounted above St. Peter's Square when he became pope—the first Marian image on the central stage of the drama of Catholicism.

DISCERNING A VOCATION is a matter of learning the truth about oneself, accepting that truth, and living that truth. That takes courage—and courage was another of the cardinal virtues that Karol Wojtyła began to display in his Dębniki years.

For it was in the apartment at Tyniecka 10 that Wojtyła, his old theatrical mentor from Wadowice, Mieczysław Kotlarczyk, and several other young people formed the **Rhapsodic Theater,** both as a means to keep alive Kotlarczyk's vision of the possibilities of avant-garde theater and as an act of resistance against the German occupation. And from "the catacombs" where their rehearsals were held, Kotlarczyk, Wojtyła, and the other members of this unique theatrical troupe risked their lives by going to homes and apartments in Kraków to perform the classics of Polish drama and recite classic Polish poetry, all in defiance of the occupation's determination that "Poland will be erased."

During one of those performances, on November 28, 1942, the Rhapsodists were performing an adaptation of Adam Mickiewicz's *Pan Tadeusz,* Poland's national poem. Outside, Nazi megaphones on a sound truck began blasting out the news of another Wehrmacht victory. Twenty-two-year-old Karol Wojtyła, by then a newly enrolled seminarian in the underground seminary of Archbishop Adam Stefan Sapieha, paid not the slightest attention to what was going on outside, continuing his recitation as if this intrusion from the principalities and powers of the age did not exist.

Thirty-seven years before he would summon the people of Poland to live in the truth, to live "as if" one were free, Karol Wojtyła had learned how to do precisely that: in Dębniki, in the crucible of a world war, and in the challenging school of vocational discernment.

Dębniki

The Dębniki neighborhood lies just across Vistula River from Wawel Hill, to the southwest of the Royal Castle and Kraków's cathedral. A working-class neighborhood when Karol Wojtyła and his father moved there in 1938, Dębniki's homes, apartments, and shops retain much of the flavor of the mid-twentieth century in the early twenty-first.

Wojtyła Apartment
ul. Tyniecka, 10

Ul. Tyniecka, where the Wojtyłas lived at number 10, is one of Dębniki's principal arteries, running alongside the Vistula and leading out of the city, where the pilgrim eventually finds the historic Benedictine monastery of Tyniec, some seven miles away. The street thus links two of the principal sites in Karol Wojtyła's spiritual itinerary: the house in which he discerned his priestly vocation, and the monastery to which he would regularly turn for spiritual renewal, including the retreat he made just prior to his ordination as a bishop in 1958.

Karol Wojtyła lived at Tyniecka 10 from the late summer of 1938 until August 6, 1944. Then, with the Gestapo trying to arrest all of the young men in Kraków to forestall a local replication of the Warsaw Uprising (which began on August 1, 1944), Wojtyła left the basement apartment his friends called "the catacombs" and, with the help of a friend, Irina Szkocka, worked his way across the city, avoiding the German patrols, to Archbishop Sapieha's residence, where he spent more than six months in hiding with the other seminarians.

The apartment is an archdiocesan museum today and contains numerous family artifacts, either originals or copies.

St. Stanisław Kostka Church
ul. Konfederacka, 6

Karol Wojtyła's parish church in Dębniki, St. Stanisław Kostka, is a ten-minute walk from the Wojtyła apartment at Tyniecka 10. Built in the early 1930s, St. Stanisław Kostka was one of Kraków's youngest parish churches when the Wojtyłas, father and son, began to worship there in 1938. Staffed then as now by the Salesians of St. John Bosco, the rectory, to the right of the church, was once home to the Salesian priests who were deported to several concentration camps during World War II, where many died as martyrs. Their witness is commemorated in a contemporary chapel to the right of the church's sanctuary. Two days after his ordination to the priesthood, Father Karol Wojtyła celebrated his first public Mass here, on November 3, 1946, an event noted in a memorial to the right of the entrance to the church.

Interior, St. Stanisław Kostka Church

Gothic in footprint and proportion, St. Stanisław Kostka was nonetheless designed and decorated in a distinctively modern, art deco style—which is somewhat surprising, given Archbishop Sapieha's traditional cast of mind. The high, vaulted nave is supported by large concrete pillars, decorated with black and white images of numerous saints—including Karol Wojtyła's baptismal patron, St. Charles Borromeo. The apse contains a mosaic image of the Risen Christ, greeted by a choir of angels in heaven.

The church is named for a Polish saint, one of the Catholic Church's principal patrons of young people. Born in 1550 to a noble family in the town of Rostkowo, in east-central Poland, Stanisław Kostka was the second of seven children. While studying with the newly founded Society of Jesus in Vienna, he discerned a Jesuit vocation, but was initially rebuffed by the Viennese Jesuit superiors, who were experiencing some backlash from noble families whose sons were committing themselves to the new order. Convinced of his own calling, Stanisław set his sights on joining the Jesuits in Rome; he finally left home after being subjected to violent attacks from his older brother. Making his way on foot to Rome, he stayed in the Bavarian town of Dillingen with Peter Canisius, another future saint, who tested the young man's vocation for a month. Persuaded that the young Pole was being called by God to a life in the Society of Jesus, Canisius sent him to the Jesuits in Rome, where he arrived on October 25, 1567, exhausted by the long and difficult journey. He seems never to have fully recovered, but died as a Jesuit novice, ten months after his arrival in the Eternal City. A beautiful marble sculpture of St. Stanisław Kostka in the old Jesuit novitiate next to Sant'Andrea al Quirinale, carved by Pierre Legros in 1705, testifies to the impression he made on the people of Rome. As a graduate student at the Pontifical University of St. Thomas Aquinas, the Angelicum, Fr. Karol Wojtyła would often stop to pray in Sant'Andrea al Quirinale on his walk from the Belgian College where he lived to the Angelicum, thus forging a link between his parish church in Kraków and his university in Rome.

St. Stanisław Kostka, a remarkable exemplar of youthful piety and commitment, was beatified in 1605 by Pope Paul V and canonized in 1726 by Pope Benedict XIII. His older brother, whose vehement attacks drove him from home, lived long enough to attend the beatification ceremony.

During World Youth Day in Rome on August 15, 2000, Pope John Paul II recalled his days as a parishioner in Dębniki: "I remember the life of the parish that I attended, named after Saint Stanisław Kostka, in Dębniki in Kraków. It was run by the Salesian Fathers, from whom I received my basic training in Christian living. I cannot forget the experience of the war and the years of work in a factory. My priestly vocation came to its full maturity during the Second World War, during the occupation of Poland. The tragedy of the war gave a particular coloring to the gradual maturing of my vocation in life. In these circumstances, I perceived a light shining ever more brightly within me: the Lord wanted me to be a priest! I remember with feeling that moment in my life when, on the morning of November 1, 1946, I was ordained a priest."

John Paul II visited St. Stanisław Kostka Church during his final pilgrimage to Kraków in 2002.

Tyranowski Apartment
ul. Różana, 11

The apartment of Jan Tyranowski (1900–1947) is a five-minute walk from St. Stanisław Kostka. Today, Tyranowski's home is a medical office. The man who introduced John Paul II to Carmelite spirituality and to the Marian theology of St. Louis Grignion de Montfort is buried and memorialized in St. Stanisław Kostka church, in a shrine just before the church's left transept. The cause for Tyranowski's beatification has been completed in Kraków and submitted to the Vatican's Congregation for the Causes of Saints.

Rakowicki Cemetery
ul. Biskupa Jana Prandoty, 1

North of **Kleparz** and the Kraków Old Town, about five and a half miles from Dębniki, Karol Wojtyła Sr., his wife, Emilia, and their son Edmund are buried in Kraków's great Rakowicki cemetery, in a family grave that includes other members of Emilia's Kaczorowski family.

The Polish custom of careful tending of the graves of the dead is on full display in the vast expanse of Rakowicki. The zenith of this noble cultural habit is the first week of November, which begins with the Solemnity of All Saints (November 1) and the Commemoration of the Faithful Departed (All Souls Day, November 2)—a week in which cemeteries throughout Poland are ablaze with votive candles, accompanied by floral displays, resting atop family graves. A nation that has had to cope with devastation and untimely death for centuries has a special place in its cultural memory for the dead, with whom the living express, through their care of graves, a powerful emotional and historical connection—a distinctive Polish embodiment of what Catholicism calls the "Communion of Saints."

Rakowicki Cemetery is Kraków's most important necropolis. First established in 1803 under Austrian rule, the cemetery was built on land purchased from the Discalced Carmelites when the city authorities, concerned about sanitation, were closing the traditional parish cemeteries that existed in virtually every parish's churchyard. The property has been enlarged five times over the last two hundred years and today covers nearly 104 acres.

Shaded by mature trees, the cemetery is a noble mix of

tombs and gravesites, featuring ubiquitous crosses, graceful Madonnas, poignant prayers, and often elaborate plots. The Wojtyła-Kaczorowski family tomb is in a section of the cemetery established in 1920, where the graves of other veterans of the Polish military may be found. Special sections of the cemetery are devoted to the fallen of the twentieth-century world wars, including dedicated plots for deceased British and German soldiers and airmen. Memorials commemorate the 1831 and 1863 revolts against Russian rule in partitioned Poland, the victims of the Holocaust, and the victims of communism. Many of the cemetery's signs are in multiple languages to facilitate foreigners finding the graves of their loved ones and ancestors.

Wojtyła-Kaczorowski Family Tomb, Rakowicki Cemetery

Rakowicki is the final resting place of many prominent Cracovians, including politicians, artists, poets, architects, sculptors, and actors. Noble families are buried together in elaborate mausoleums, while sprawling plots with identical markers denote the graves of members of religious communities.

Pope John Paul II visited the cemetery during each of his pastoral pilgrimages to Poland. His visits are commemorated in the cemetery by a large statue of the Pope kneeling in prayer, unveiled shortly after his death in 2005. [C.G.]

The Jagiellonian University

Faith and Reason

For sixty-seven years, from his matriculation in 1938 until his death in 2005, the **Jagiellonian University** held a special place in the affections of Karol Wojtyła, St. John Paul II.

His own studies there were conducted in difficult circumstances. He spent a brief freshman year studying Polish

Plus ratio quam vis, *Aula Magna of the Collegium Maius*

philology and literature before the Nazis closed the university in the late fall of 1939 and deported 184 faculty members to the Sachsenhausen concentration camp. When the Jagiellonian defiantly reconstituted itself during the war years as an underground institution of higher learning, the young worker-student took clandestine courses from Jagiellonian professors in pursuit of his first degree. After the occupation, when the Jagiellonian emerged from the underground and something resembling normal academic life resumed in the fall of 1945, Wojtyła, by then a seminarian, did three semesters of first-level theological study at the university, prior to his ordination to the priesthood on November 1, 1946. Then, after completing a first doctorate in Rome, he did a second doctorate at the Jagiellonian in 1951–53, the "habilitation" degree that qualified him as a professor—the last such degree conferred by the university's centuries-old theology department before it was shut down by Poland's communist government in an act of cultural vandalism that Wojtyła deplored for decades.

Yet despite these unusual circumstances, the Jagiellonian University remained throughout Wojtyła's life a primary symbol of Poland's rich intellectual culture, and thus an essential part of Polish nationhood. For Karol Wojtyła, a "nation" was more than a matter of ethnicity and territory, its reality defined by lines on a map. A "nation" was an expression of culture, of a people's language and literature, its science, music, and fine arts—and, of course, its religious convictions. In a certain sense, nations had souls (or, as he would put it philosophically, "subjectivity"), and while the soul of Poland could be experienced in famous religious shrines such as the Jasna Góra monastery in Częstochowa, home of the Black

Madonna, or **Kalwaria Zebrzydowska,** near his hometown, Poland's soul also lived, in a distinctive way, in the Jagiellonian University.

POLAND'S SOUL HAD everything to do with Poland's survival, in Karol Wojtyła's view. Located on a flat plain between two expansive, often aggressive, and usually conflicted great powers, Prussia and Russia, Poland was a natural invasion route, a battlefield-in-waiting. The surrounding neighborhood, which eventually consumed Poland in 1795, seemed to confirm the modern view that material power is decisive in history: the power of natural and financial resources transformed into military prowess determines the fate of nations. Poland's tenacious grip on its own national idea after the Third Polish Partition in 1795 destroyed its independence as a state; its political resurrection in 1918; its ability to withstand, for fifty years, both a brutal Nazi occupation and the communist usurpation of its national identity and its liberties; its central role in the Revolution of 1989 and the collapse of European communism—all these facts of history suggested to Wojtyła the insufficiency (to put it gently) of the materialist view of history and power. Poland was a reminder to the world that there is more to history and power than brute force; the human spirit can bend the course of history in nobler directions. Culture drives history, over the long haul.

KAROL WOJTYŁA KNEW at least some of this from the lessons in Polish history taught by his father. Those lessons were amplified by his experience of the Jagiellonian University: not only by the university's skill and courage in surviving the cultural and intellectual wreckage wrought by two totalitarian powers, each based on false ideas about human beings, their nature and destiny, but by the Jagiellonian's history and its moral commitments. That history included theologians of note, including Paweł Włodkovic, a late medieval exponent of what the twentieth century would call "religious freedom," and great scientists such as Copernicus, who reshaped humanity's understanding of the cosmos. As for the university's moral commitments, those were driven home to every teacher and student by the Latin inscription over the entrance to the *Aula Magna,* the Great Hall of the **Collegium Maius,** the university's most famous building and the site, for centuries, of its most solemn academic celebrations: PLUS RATIO QUAM VIS (Reason rather than force).

To a brilliant young Pole deprived of a normal academic life by the forces of irrationality wedded to overwhelming material force—forces that denied his humanity and scorned his national culture—the Jagiellonian University motto *Plus ratio quam vis* might have seemed romantic foolishness: this was obviously *not* how the world worked. Yet throughout the Nazi occupation of Poland and during the communist tyranny that followed, Karol Wojtyła never lost his conviction that *Plus ratio quam vis* expressed a deep truth of the human condition. Reason really *is* better than force, because reason is an expression of the human person's spiritual nature, which the proponents of brute force as the engine of history deny. To stand for reason, then, is to stand fast for some essential truths

Arcaded courtyard, Collegium Maius

about human beings—the truths that there is more to us than matter, that we are not just congealed stardust, that our existence is not an accident of impersonal cosmic biochemical forces, that we are animated by souls, and that our noblest aspirations are spiritual.

KAROL WOJTYŁA DEVOTED much of his intellectual life as a philosopher to the defense of the idea that there are deep truths built into the world and into us, truths that we can know by reason. A decade after he completed his habilitation doctorate at the Jagiellonian University, he tried to demonstrate the human capacity to grasp the truth of things through an analysis of human moral agency in *Person and Act,* his most important philosophical work. Modern philosophy, Wojtyła believed, tended to lock human beings into what another Polish philosopher, Wojciech Chudy, would later call the "trap of reflection": thinking about thinking about thinking, rather than thinking about the truth of things. This radical subjectivism, this getting lost inside one's own consciousness, seemed to Wojtyła one of the roots of modernity's discontents—even its lethal passions—for the history of the twentieth century had demonstrated beyond dispute that ideas have consequences. By reestablishing a tether between thought and the world, between reality and the moral life, he hoped to make a philosophical contribution to the rescue of Western humanism, and to the building of a world that had rediscovered the truth of *Plus ratio quam vis.*

Wojtyła's conviction that human beings could know the truth, and that in knowing the truth they would be set free in the deepest meaning of human liberation, had biblical as well as philosophical roots. True, his early philosophical studies, done in the dim light of the night shift at the **Solvay chemical factory** during the war, had shown him that there was a structure to reality, a rational order of things that made sense of the world. But his belief in the human capacity to grasp the truth of things was also formed by his Christian faith and by his lifelong immersion in the Bible, which helped him "read" the world through biblical as well as philosophical lenses.

As a close student of the Bible, and especially of John's Gospel, Karol Wojtyła reflected for decades on the meaning of the Prologue to that most theologically dense of the four

Jan Matejko, Copernicus—Conversation with God, *Aula of the Collegium Novum*

canonical gospels: "In the beginning was the Word, and the Word was with God, and the Word was God. He was in the beginning with God; all things were made through him, and without him was not anything made that was made. In him was life, and the life was the light of men" (John 1:1–4). Read in parallel with the opening lines of the Old Testament—"In the beginning, God created the heavens and the earth" (Genesis 1:1)—the Prologue to John's Gospel was a biblical affirmation that, in creating the world through the Word, the *Logos,* God had encoded a divine rationality into the creation. Creation was neither random nor irrational. The God of the Bible had created an intelligible world, a world replete with meaning, full of truths that the human mind could grasp. And in the beginning, by giving human beings dominion over the creation and giving Adam the power to name all living things, the God of the Bible had indicated that he had no intention of keeping his noblest creation, the human person, in ignorance: the world was a vast subject for human beings to explore, to ponder, and to understand.

For Karol Wojtyła, then, the intellectual life, the life of the mind, was a facet of the spiritual life. What the twenty-first century calls "spirituality" is often set against reason, or, at the very least, seems primarily concerned with feeling. Wojtyła, a man of warmth and deep compassion, certainly knew the truth of the motto on Blessed John Henry Newman's cardinalatial coat of arms: *Cor ad cor loquitur* (Heart speaks to heart). As a faithful son of the Jagiellonian University, however, he also knew that the intellectual life and the spiritual life do not exist in hermetically sealed containers, as if reason has nothing to do with belief or with friendship with Jesus Christ. The act of faith must be both free and informed to be true to itself; theology, the science of faith, is a genuine intellectual discipline, not a first cousin to mythology or psychology.

IN WOJTYŁA'S VIEW of the world and history, the Jagiellonian University, and other such enterprises throughout the West, were by-products of the fruitful interaction, over three millennia, between Athens and Jerusalem: between the conviction, first planted in Western civilization by the Greeks, that human reason could get at the truth of things, and the conviction, a gift to the West from the Jewish people, that the ultimate foundation for the world's intelligibility is God the Creator, who made all things and saw that they were good. Jerusalem and Athens, in other words, were two of the pillars on which Western civilization, and indeed Poland, were built.

Throughout the nineteenth century, however, acids were at work in Western intellectual life—acids that would eventually dissolve (or at last severely weaken) the connection between faith and reason, between Jerusalem and Athens. Jerusalem was the first target. Nineteenth-century Western high culture threw the God of the Bible over the side of history, claiming that only a humanity rid of religious superstition and tutored by the empiricism of the scientific method could be a mature and free humanity. Revelation, it was claimed, was the mortal enemy of reason.

Yet as things turned out, the loss of "Jerusalem" had a disastrous effect on reason. Throw away the convictions that human reason is ultimately a reflection of the divine reason, and that the divine reason has encoded intelligibility into the world, and it turns out that reason, by itself, cannot sustain itself. Left to its own devices, reason gets lost in that "trap of reflection," or, worse, deteriorates into irrationality. Marry irrationality to technology and the result was the Nazi blitzkrieg, which shut down the Jagiellonian University and murdered its professors. Marry an ultramundane and materialistic rationality to technology and the result was communism, which denied positions on the Jagiellonian University faculty to men and women of faith.

The victory of imperfect democracies over pluperfect

tyrannies in World War II and the Cold War finished German National Socialism and communism as viable historical projects. But the severing of Athens and Jerusalem continued to have deleterious effects in the West. Reason's lack of confidence in its own ability to get at the truth of things with any certainty led, in the late twentieth century, to a postmodernism that was prepared to concede that there was "your truth" and "my truth" but refused to recognize anything as *the* truth. And that, too, was a prescription for trouble, and for violations of the moral maxim *Plus ratio quam vis.* For if there is only *your* truth and *my* truth, and neither one of us recognizes anything as *the* truth, then what happens when your truth and my truth come into conflict? Absent any standard of reason—*the* truth—by which to settle the argument, one of two things happens: either I impose my power on you, or you impose your power on me. Pope Benedict XVI would call this the "dictatorship of relativism"; in the early decades of the twenty-first century, it remains a cultural and political threat to free societies throughout the world.

KNOWING ALL OF this, John Paul II returned to his Jagiellonian roots, the principle of *Plus ratio quam vis,* and the fruitful interaction of Athens and Jerusalem in his 1998 encyclical, *Fides et Ratio* (Faith and Reason). In the modern cultural history of the West, *Fides et Ratio* represents something of an intellectual earthquake: two and a half centuries after Voltaire called for crushing the "infamy," the Catholic Church, in the name of reason and its prerogatives, here was the Catholic Church, embodied by a Polish pope, positioning itself as the chief institutional defender of reason and its prerogatives in the third millennium. While some philosophers remained caught in the wilderness of mirrors that was the trap of reflection, and Western culture as a whole flailed about in the quicksand pits of "your truth" and "my truth," the universal pastor of the Catholic Church calmly and confidently defended the capacity of human reason to grasp the truth of things, including the moral truth of things.

And John Paul went further still. Rather than seeing reason as a mere adjunct to religion, the Catholic Church believed that reason was essential to faith. Reason purifies faith, purging it of any elements of superstition and allowing Christians to live the apostolic admonition to give an "account for the hope that is in you" (1 Peter 3:15). By the same token, faith could be of service to reason: reason informed by faith is amplified and enlarged by faith, so that reason does not set its sights too low. Athens once again in conversation with Jerusalem is Athens in its full glory.

"Faith and reason," John Paul wrote in 1998, "are like two wings on which the human spirit rises to the contemplation of the truth." And in that contemplation, restless human beings can find a place of repose that is also a place of expanding horizons: we can choose "to enter the truth, to make a home under the shade of Wisdom and to dwell there."

THE COMPLEX AND rich interior life of John Paul II included what might be called a "humanistic soul." It was the dimension of his soul formed by his conviction that the crisis of the late modern world was rooted in a crisis in Western humanism: a project that had gone off the rails in the second half of the second millennium, when false ideas about the human person led to evils that sought to destroy institutions of humanistic learning such as the Jagiellonian University. Yet the humanistic tradition was not wrong, Karol Wojtyła knew, in lifting up the human person as a creature capable of knowledge and nobility. By helping reconvene the conversation between Athens and Jerusalem, between faith and reason, the Catholic Church could help heal the terrible wounds caused by the collapse of the western humanistic project into various destructive forces. That was the conviction that a son of the Jagiellonian University brought with him to Rome on his election as that city's bishop in 1978. It was a conviction that began to take shape in the university he revered for more than six decades.

That conviction about the healing and ennobling capacities of faith purified by reason and reason amplified by faith was a gift from the Jagiellonian University to the world, offered across the globe by the university's most distinguished twentieth-century graduate.

The Jagiellonian University

A glance at the history of the Jagiellonian University is a good way to gauge the health of Kraków at any given point since the university's establishment in 1364. The university's openings and closures, its changes in curriculum and languages of instruction, its treatment of professors and students, its fires and expansions mirror the drama unfolding in the city over six and a half centuries. As the city's fortunes went, so did the university's.

The university was founded in the mid-fourteenth century during the reign of King Kazimierz III ("the Great"), at the beginning of Kraków's rise to economic, spiritual, and political prominence. In need of lawyers and other educated men to aid his efforts to restructure the country and regularize its administration, the reforming king received permission from Pope Urban V to open what was known originally as the Academy of Kraków; it was the second institution of higher learning to be established in central Europe, Prague's Charles University having opened in 1348. After the premature death of King Kazimierz in 1370, his successor, King Louis of Hungary, showed little interest in the enterprise, allowing it to go to seed.

The Academy was restored to prominence by Louis's successor and younger daughter, Queen Jadwiga, who was crowned *Rex Poloniae* (King of Poland) in 1384 because of a Polish law proscribing a regnant queen. Jadwiga and her Lithuanian husband, Władysław Jagiełło, petitioned Pope Boniface IX, then in Avignon, to reestablish the defunct Academy. The youthful queen died in 1399, a month after giving birth to a daughter, but the Academy was reestablished in 1400 with the aid of the large fortune Jadwiga bequeathed to the university.

The university's status soared in the fifteenth and sixteenth centuries, the golden age of both the school and the city. Virtually the entire noble class of Poland was educated at the Academy, in an innovative intellectual atmosphere (the university was the first in Europe to have independent chairs of mathematics and astronomy) and a culturally pluralistic environment that included students from Lithuania, Germany, Russia, Hungary, Bohemia, and Spain—among them Mikołaj Kopernik (Copernicus), who studied liberal arts at the Academy of Kraków from 1491 to 1495.

Two events in the sixteenth century, one religious and the other legal, had a marked effect on higher education in Kraków. The theological and, ultimately, ecclesiastical divisions of the Reformation resulted in the closure of the Academy's German and Hungarian dormitories; thereafter the Academy's students were almost exclusively Polish and Lithuanian. Changes in the laws setting the academic qualifications required for noblemen to hold important public offices were drastically modified, making university study unnecessary for many of those with political ambitions.

The Academy of Kraków limped through the next two centuries, facing the challenges of invasions, fires, and disease, but it was not until the Third Polish Partition of 1795 that the university was threatened with extinction. Viewed by the new Austrian authorities as a potential threat to their rule, given its reputation as a center of revolutionary and anti-Austrian agitation, the Academy might have been shut down but for the efforts of two influential professors, Jan Sniadecki and Józef Bogucki, who were, in the event, able to persuade those in charge in Vienna to keep the Academy open—even though the official language of instruction was changed to German and Polish nationalism on campus was suppressed.

In the mid-nineteenth century, a new golden age dawned for Cracovian higher education, as the Academy (which had been renamed the Jagiellonian University in 1861) gradually reacquired its rights of self-governance—and the right of its professors to teach in Polish. In the mid-nineteenth century the university improved its infrastructure and added to its roster of academic chairs. Women were admitted in 1894 to study pharmacology; the other constituent schools of the university gradually followed suit, the last being the law school, which admitted its first women students in 1918.

The Jagiellonian University expanded considerably after the recovery of Polish independence at the end of World War I, even as it struggled with the political divisions of the Second Polish Republic and the devastating effects of the Great Depression. Yet nothing in the Jagiellonian's previous five and a half centuries of academic and cultural life compared to the devastation wrought by the Second World War.

The university was closed; its property was destroyed, looted, or sent to Germany. On November 6, 1939, the Nazis called a meeting of all professors to discuss "German plans for Polish education" at the Aula in the Collegium Novum. The 184 teachers who came as ordered were summarily arrested and deported to Sachsenhausen in an operation code-named *Sonderaktion Krakau*—a dramatic example of the German effort to decapitate Poland by eliminating its cultural leaders. During the war, thirty-four Jagiellonian professors and staff were killed at Sachsenhausen, Dachau, and Auschwitz, while another fourteen sons of the Jagiellonian, professors and graduates serving as reserve officers, were murdered by the Soviet secret police, the NKVD, in the Katyn forest massacres.

The university quickly reconstituted itself as an underground institution of higher learning, which educated some eight hundred students during World War II. With the Germans driven from Kraków by the Red Army in January 1945, the university emerged from underground, and within a month of the war's end, more than five thousand students registered for classes. In the aftermath of the war, many professors from other parts of Poland found employment at the Jagiellonian, their own universities having been reduced to rubble or incorporated into the Soviet Union.

After an initial breathing space of some three years, the shadow of Polish Stalinism fell over the university in 1948, with the Communist Party, the ironically styled Polish United Workers' Party, controlling every aspect of university life, eliminating

*Memorial to murdered
professors, Collegium Novum*

some departments, and dismissing professors regarded as politically dangerous (i.e., intellectually independent). The workers' revolts of 1956 across central and eastern Europe led to a political thaw in Poland, with the university regaining its rights of self-government.

Thirty years after the Stalinist clampdown on its activities, the university saw one of its graduates elected as the 264th Bishop of Rome. Today, in the twenty-first century, the Jagiellonian University retains its rank as one of Poland's premier institutions of higher learning.

Collegium Maius
ul. Jagiellonska, 15

The Collegium Maius, or Great College, is the university's oldest building and today houses the Jagiellonian University Museum.

During the university's first centuries, professors' quarters were located upstairs, while lecture halls, the library, and the communal halls were all downstairs. The rooms of one famous professor, St. Jan Kanty, were transformed into a chapel to commemorate the saint's life and service to the university. The graceful brick structure of the Collegium Maius features grand arches and a large courtyard, in which may be seen the arms of some of the university's most prominent personalities, including St. John Paul II.

The museum includes a treasure trove of medieval instruments, paintings, collectables, furniture, coins, and medals. Notable among the collectables are the rectors' Gothic maces and the Jagiellonian globe; crafted in the early sixteenth century, it is the oldest existing globe to show the Americas.

The museum leads into the Aula Magna of the Collegium Maius, through a door over which is carved the motto PLUS RATIO QUAM VIS.

Collegium Novum
ul. Gołębia, 24

The Collegium Novum, or New College, is the main administrative building of the Jagiellonian University. Built on the site of the university's Jerusalem College, which was destroyed in the 1850 fire that did severe damage to Kraków's Old Town, the neo-Gothic Collegium Novum was raised between 1883 and 1887. Although architect Feliks Księżarski was commissioned to match the style of the Collegium Maius, his work is better understood as a replica of German and Austrian models, the effects of which may be seen in the college's magnificent main staircase, strikingly similar to the staircase in Vienna's Town Hall.

The completion of the Collegium Novum coincided with celebrations marking the fifth centenary of the university's restoration under King Władysław Jagiełło and Queen Jadwiga, and despite Austrian fears of patriotic demonstrations for the restoration of Poland's independence, the College was dedicated with representatives of all three parts of partitioned Poland present.

Today, the Collegium Novum houses the office of the Rector of the Jagiellonian University, along with departmental offices, the university bursary, and a great Hall (or Aula) where inaugurations and graduation ceremonies take place. The Aula

Collegium Novum

boasts a beamed and coffered ceiling, its walls decorated with portraits of the university's founders and rectors by the great nineteenth-century Polish painter Jan Matejko, himself the founder of the **Kraków Academy of Fine Arts.** Among the canvases is Matejko's *Copernicus: Conversation with God.* A portrait of Austrian emperor Franz Joseph hung in the Aula until 1918, when it was shredded by students demanding an independent Poland. John Paul II's address to the university on June 22, 1983, in which he recounted his personal history at the Jagiellonian and urged the university to be true to its origins, is commemorated by a portrait near the door.

The *Sonderaktion Krakau,* and the Jagiellonian professors who died during World War II are remembered on a plaque outside the Aula.

St. Anne's Collegiate Church
ul. św. Anny, 11

Like St. Mary the Virgin in Oxford, the Collegiate Church of St. Anne has long served as the Jagiellonian University's parish church.

First mentioned in 1381, the current church is the third to sit upon this site in the Old Town's University Tract. The first, a wooden church, was built in the fourteenth century, adjacent to a synagogue and *mikveh* (ritual bath); it burned down in 1407 during an anti-Jewish riot. The second church on the site was built in the Gothic style by King Władysław Jagiełło, who formally attached the church to the university, which was

Ashes of Jerzy Ciesielski, Collegiate Church of St. Anne

Tomb of St. Jan Kanty,
Collegiate Church of
St. Anne

permitted to appoint its priest; St. Anne's was given the rank of a collegiate church by a charter dated October 27, 1535.

In the seventeenth century, professors from the Academy, supported by King Jan III Sobieski (himself a graduate of the Academy), decided to build a more splendid church to accommodate the growing number of pilgrims who wished to venerate the university's late professor and patron saint, St. Jan Kanty. Following the designs of Sobieski's chief architect, the Polonized Dutchman Tylman van Gameren, the new church, completed in 1705, was modeled after Sant'Andrea della Valle in Rome (which had been completed in 1650). Like Sant'Andrea della Valle, St. Anne's is fashioned in a high baroque style and features a lavish dome and facade similar to its Roman prototype.

The church's rich interior, bathed in natural light, and the soaring heights of its ceilings and three interior aisles create a powerful impression. The interior decoration was the work

*Collegiate Church of
St. Anne*

of the Italian master Baldassare Fontana, with the polychromy painted by the Italian brothers Carlo and Innocente Monti, and a Swede, Karl Dankwart of Nysa. The dome rests on spherically shaped pendentives depicting the four cardinal virtues: Prudence, Justice, Fortitude, and Temperance. The central painting of St. Anne at the high altar is the work of Sobieski's court painter, Jerzy Siemiginowski-Eleuter. The eighteenth-century paintings of the life of St. Anne in the sanctuary stalls were done by the Polish baroque artist Szymon Częchowicz.

The tomb of St. Jan Kanty (1390–1473), a graduate of the Academy of Kraków and later theology professor in the university, is in the right transept. His coffin rests on the shoulders of four allegorical figures, representing the academic disciplines of his day: Theology, Medicine, Philosophy, and Law. An annual procession of professors and students to the saint's tomb on October 20 honors Jan Kanty's Polish feast day. To the left of St. Jan Kanty's tomb is a wall niche containing the ashes of the Servant of God Jerzy Ciesielski, a close friend of Karol Wojtyła and his instructor in the art of kayaking, whose beatification cause is under consideration. Ciesielski, who served as an altar boy at St. Anne's, is also commemorated by a bronze plaque at the rear of the church.

To the left of the high altar is a modest monument to Copernicus, the university's most famous graduate. The Servant of God Jan Pietraszko, a priest of Kraków who conducted a highly successful campus ministry from the church throughout the 1950s and who later served as an auxiliary bishop under Cardinal Karol Wojtyła, is buried beneath the altar in the left transept; the cause for Bishop Pietraszko's beatification is also under way.

Masses in aid of the beatification causes of Jerzy Ciesielski and Bishop Jan Pietraszko are celebrated weekly in the church. [C.G.]

World War II

*The Mystery of Evil and
the Dignity of Work*

The experience of World War II was decisive in forming the man who became Pope St. John Paul II.

The brutality of the Nazi occupation of Poland was compounded by its irrationality. In the *General Gouvernement* (those German-occupied parts of Poland's prewar territory that had not been absorbed into the Third Reich, like Wadowice and the surrounding region, nor incorporated into the Soviet Union, like Lwów and other parts of Galicia), the rule of law ceased to exist in any meaningful sense. Because Nazi racial ideology considered Poles as Slavic *Untermenschen*, lower life-forms, the occupation treated Poles as a mass labor force, to be kept alive at a minimum of expense until the Poles died of exhaustion or starvation. Poland would "be erased," according to the Nazi governor-general, Hans Frank. But until the erasure was completed, Poles had no rights that the occupying power was bound to acknowledge.

Thus a Wehrmacht officer, SS officer, or Gestapo agent, taking offense that a Pole did not step off a sidewalk and into the street to make way for him, could shoot down the

Katyn memorial cross, Church of St. Giles

offending *Untermensch* with impunity. Life, or at least Polish life, was not merely cheap in the *General Gouvernement*; death was a constant presence and could come randomly and unexpectedly—as it did one day to Jerzy Zachuta, one of Karol Wojtyła's fellow clandestine seminarians, who didn't show up one morning to help serve Archbishop Sapieha's Mass, and whose name appeared later that day on a roster of Poles to be shot.

Life in the *General Gouvernement* between September 1939 and January 1945 was thus life under unremitting and intense pressure: one never knew whether one would be alive the next evening, much less the following year. Different people reacted to those pressures in different ways. Some took up arms, hiding in the dense Polish forests and conducting guerilla raids against the Germans. Some became attracted to communism, in the hope of building a postwar secular utopia. Some fell into despair and simply wasted away, while others, abandoning hope, took their own lives. Many, perhaps the majority, just tried to survive, muddling through from day to day while constantly aware of the possibility of random annihilation. Like the immense natural forces beneath the crust of the earth that produce destructive earthquakes, volcanic eruptions, and lava flows, the Polish people during World War II were subjected to irrational and often lethal pressures over which they had no control.

Yet those titanic pressures beneath the earth's surface also form something else: they form diamonds, the hardest, clearest substance known to our science. That is what happened to Karol Wojtyła under the pressures of World War II and the irrational brutality of the German occupation: he became a kind of diamond, able to cut through substances that seemed impermeable—such as the Berlin Wall—and able to refract light in a singularly luminous way. Four decades after the war, the young man who found his vocation in the cauldron of World War II and who had become Pope John Paul II met Elena Bonner, the wife of Russian physicist and human rights campaigner Andrei Sakharov, who had come to Rome while her husband was still forbidden to travel by the Soviet authorities. Elena Bonner was a very tough woman, steeled by her own experience of totalitarian brutality. Yet after two hours with John Paul II, she was in tears, saying to a friend who met her after her private audience, "He's the most remarkable man I've ever met. He is all light. He is a source of light." That light, John Paul II would have insisted, was not his, but the light of

Memorial Cross,
KL-Płaszów

the divine mercy. It was, however, light refracted through the diamond-like character of Karol Wojtyła, which was forged under the relentless pressures of World War II and the German occupation of Kraków.

EVIL AND SATAN might have seemed abstractions in the catechism taught to young Karol Wojtyła in Wadowice. They were not abstractions in Kraków during the Second World War, which forced the young student-worker to confront the *mysterium iniquitatis,* the mystery of evil, head-on.

Evil, the catechism had taught him, was a failure to conform oneself to the divine will, which was made known in the Ten Commandments and the moral teaching of the Church. That was simple enough to grasp as an abstract proposition, and it seemed confirmed by personal experience: doing what is right leads one toward happiness, while doing what one knows is wrong rings the bell of conscience and leads toward self-reproach. What World War II taught Karol Wojtyła was that this abstract "failure to conform one's will to the will of God" could so deeply warp human personalities that men and women eagerly gave their lives to evil systems and their degradation of the human person.

That dimension of the *mysterium iniquitatis* was on lethal display in Kraków at **KL-Płaszów**, the concentration camp made famous by *Schindler's List*, and a few dozen miles away at the **Auschwitz complex**, where, in the gas chambers pioneered at Auschwitz I and perfected at Auschwitz II–Birkenau, more than a million human beings were killed for no other reason than that they offended Nazi racial ideology or were otherwise considered enemies of the Third Reich. And the killing was done as a kind of industrial process, the mass production of death: German firms bid for contracts to develop and manufacture Zyklon-B, the lethal agent used to gas hundreds to death at a time, while other firms worked hard to design crematoria that could "handle" thousands of corpses a day—corpses that had already been stripped of what could be useful for the German war machine, including hair and gold dental fillings.

Even the SS found the commandant of KL-Płaszów, Amon Göth, too much to take, and he was eventually suspended from his duties. But it is difficult to walk through the barren fields that are all that remain of KL-Płaszów today, much less through the vast expanse of Auschwitz II–Birkenau, with its row upon row of huts where the victims of the Holocaust awaited execution, without concluding that evil is no abstraction and that Satan is far more than a literary image for wickedness. The photos and films of the famous railroad tracks into Birkenau, where prisoners were quickly separated into those who would die immediately and those who would die a little later, show educated and presumably cultured German officers, including physicians, consigning men, women, and children to immediate death—or worse, to gruesome "medical experiments"—as a matter of course, and without any visible displays of regret. Looking at those grainy pictures and newsreels, it is not easy to explain the phenomenon of Nazism and what it did to its adherents simply by reference to historical circumstances—any more than it is possible to explain, by appeal to revolutionary imperatives, how Soviet NKVD agents could shoot twenty-three thousand Polish officers in the back of the head, one by one, in the Katyn forests. The appeal to Satan and his minions as a causal factor in large historical events should be deployed with great care. But at KL-Płaszów and Auschwitz-Birkenau, that appeal is virtually unavoidable to anyone with a biblical sense of the world and of history.

Evil and Satan could not be abstractions to Karol Wojtyła after the experience of World War II. The question then became, what is the proper response to evil, and to the Evil One? They must be resisted, of course. But how? In the cauldron of the Second World War, in which the dignity of the human person was trampled upon in the most lethal ways imaginable, Karol Wojtyła took the decision to resist evil with good. That was one purpose of the Rhapsodic Theater: to mount a cultural resistance to the Nazi determination to obliterate Poland and the Poles by keeping the idea of "Poland" alive through performances of its greatest literary works. Later, as a priest in Kraków, Father Karol Wojtyła would fight evil, the Evil One, and their assault on human dignity by creating zones of freedom in which young men and women could unveil the truth of their humanity in the light of the Gospel—and then go out to live lives of integrity in their families and professions. Later still, as pope, John Paul II would fight evil and the Evil One by clarion calls to respect the innate dignity and inalienable rights of every human person, beginning with the first right, the right of religious freedom.

During the Second World War, Karol Wojtyła was surrounded by the *mysterium iniquitatis,* red in tooth and claw. His response to the mystery of evil was to embrace the cross of Christ as a priest of the Catholic Church, spending out his life in defense of the dignity of others. Living out that vocation brought him, quite unexpectedly, to the Chair of St. Peter. Once there, he lifted up as exemplars of the capacity of good to resist, and ultimately triumph over, evil, a man and a woman, both killed at Auschwitz, whom he canonized as saints: Father Maximilian Kolbe, the Franciscan "martyr of charity" in the starvation bunker at Auschwitz, and Edith Stein, Sister Teresa Benedicta of the Cross, the distinguished philosopher, Catholic convert, and Carmelite nun, murdered in one of the early gas chambers in retaliation for the Dutch bishops' condemnation of Nazi anti-Semitism.

JOHN PAUL II was the first pope in a very long time to have spent years as a manual laborer—another facet of his unique biography that was a direct result of World War II. Being the

Zakrzówek quarry

philosopher and poet he was, however, Wojtyła did not consider hard, physical work as something one did and then forgot
about. Rather, it was something one did and then reflected
upon in the light of faith and reason—something that could be
turned into an inspiration for art, philosophy, and theology.

Breaking rocks at the **Zakrzówek quarry** was Karol
Wojtyła's first experience of grueling, backbreaking manual
labor. He came away from it toughened physically and deepened spiritually. His relationship with uneducated working-
men and his respect for the steadiness with which they bore
their burdens to support their families reinforced in him the
conviction that there was an inherent dignity in every human
person, even as it helped prepare him for a priestly ministry
in which not every one of his congregants would be an intellectual like himself. It also taught him that dignity, and the
meaning built into work by the Creator, could be found in

what seemed the uninspiring drudgery of dynamiting and then breaking up chunks of limestone.

A decade and a half after the war, in a poem called "The Quarry," Wojtyła looked back on his wartime experiences of manual labor and tried to tease the deeper meaning out of them:

> Listen, when cadences of knocking hammers so much
>   their own
> I transfer into our inner life, to test the strength of each
>   blow—
> Listen: electric current cuts through a river of rock—
> Then the thought grows in me day after day,
> The whole greatness of this work dwells inside a man.

Here was an insight, first expressed in blank verse, that the former quarryman would later develop as pope in a remarkable social encyclical on the meaning of work, *Laborem Exercens,* which John Paul II published in 1981. "On Human Work" was deeply influenced by John Paul's wartime experience, and the moral and spiritual conclusions about work he drew from that experience. One of those conclusions involved a happy inversion of a traditional approach to work in Catholic piety and catechesis, according to which work was a punishment for original sin. Had Adam and Eve not made a mess of things in the Garden, as this line of teaching went, their descendants would not have had to work. This seemed not quite right to Karol Wojtyła, the former worker-seminarian.

Work, he taught in *Laborem Exercens,* was an essential component of a fully human life, for, viewed through a biblical optic on the world, human work was our participation in God's ongoing creation of the world. (The latter was a notion John Paul took from Thomas Aquinas, who famously taught that if God wanted to end the world, God would not have to do something; rather, God would have to *stop* doing something.) However boring or tedious, difficult or dangerous, human work has a profound spiritual dimension. And because our work is a participation in God's "work," human work is capable of amplifying the dignity of the human person. To work, John Paul II taught in *Laborem Exercens,* is not just to make more. To work, and to understand one's work as a privileged participation in the divine creativity, is to *be* more: to be more fully the image of God that is our deepest and truest identity.

THREE DECADES AFTER Wojtyła wrote "The Quarry" and a year before the publication of *Laborem Exercens,* John Paul II's friend and fellow philosopher, Józef Tischner, preached one of the twentieth century's greatest sermons at a Mass during the First Solidarity Congress, held in Gdańsk in September 1981. Tischner combined the rugged good humor and patriotism of a Polish highlander with a first-class intellect. So he began his sermon, which beautifully reflected the thought of John Paul II, with some essential truth-telling to the men and women deliberating the future of the communist world's first independent, self-governing trade union. Father Tischner didn't tell the thousands assembled in Gdańsk that they were heroes for having formed Solidarity, although he, and they, understood that they had already done something historic. He told them they could be men and women of destiny and national renewal only if they faced the hard truth about their lives—the truth of what communism had done to their work, and to them:

> Polish work is sick. That is the reason why we are here—because Polish work is sick. It is as great as the Vistula [River], but equally polluted. Today we ask, why is it sick? It is not easy to answer this question, but certain facts are obvious. Instead of enhancing reciprocity, instead of being a sphere for man, work in Poland became a sphere for disagreement, dispute, or even treason. The waters of the Vistula are dirty. The waters of the Vistula are even bloody. We are here to clean the waters of the Vistula. Let us work on work, so that work can again become a sphere for agreement, accord, and peace.

Curing Polish work (and, by extension, Poland) of its communist-inflicted sickness was not just a matter of politics, Tischner continued. Nor was it simply a matter of adjusting the mechanisms of labor and industry, such that the old joke about Polish labor during the communist period—"We pretend to work and they pretend to pay us"—was rendered a thing of the past. The cure was, fundamentally, a matter of the spirit, of national cultural renewal. It was a matter of recovering the truth about Poland's history and culture, as John Paul II had challenged his countrymen to do during his first papal pilgrimage to his homeland in June 1979. It was a matter of conversion:

We must look at the issue [of work] from above, like looking from the peaks of the Tatras, where the waters of the Vistula have their beginning. The very liturgy of the Mass encourages us to do this.... This bread and wine will become in a moment the body and blood of the Son of God. This has a deep meaning.... Were it not for human work, there would be no bread and wine. Without bread and wine, there would not be among us the Son of God. God does not come to us through a creation of nature alone, holy trees, water, or fire. God comes to us through the first creation of culture—bread and wine. Work that creates bread and wine paves the way toward God. But every work has a part in this work. Our work, too. In this way our work, the work of each of us, paves the way to God . . .

Our concern is with the independence of Polish work. The word "independence" must be understood properly. It does not aim at breaking away from others. Work is reciprocity, it is agreement, it is multifaceted dependence. Work creates a communion. . . .

We are living history. A living history means one that bears fruit. Christ has said, "Let the dead bury their dead" (Matthew 8:22). Thus, let us do the same. Let us become occupied with bearing fruit.

A long and complex road runs from the limestone quarry at Zakrzówek to the shipyards in Gdańsk. Along that road, however, important truths about work, its inherent dignity, and its spiritual dimension can be found: at the beginning, at the destination, and along the way.

The World War II Sites

The sites associated with Karol Wojtyła's World War II experience are scattered around Kraków; the Auschwitz-Birkenau complex is thirty-five miles to the west of the city, in and outside the Polish town of Oswięcim.

Zakrzówek Quarry
Near the intersection of ul. Norymberska and ul. Wyłom

The quarry is now a small lake and is privately held. Views of the former limestone quarry can be found along the perimeter roads surrounding it, along which a small plaque commemorates John Paul II's work as a quarryman and dynamiter during World War II.

John Paul II memorial, Solvay chemical works

Solvay chemical works

Solvay Chemical Factory
ul. Zakopiańska, 62

The vast Solvay chemical works in the Borek Fałęcki district of Kraków no longer exist; the area once occupied by the plants where Karol Wojtyła worked during the Second World War is now home to shopping malls and a large movie complex. One of the old Solvay buildings remains, directly alongside the road to Zakopane. Wojtyła's work at Solvay is commemorated there by a bronze memorial.

Kazimierz, KL-Płaszów, and the Schindler Factory

Kraków was home to as many as eighty thousand Jews prior to the Second World War. At the war's end, only six thousand had survived.

The evils of anti-Semitism that have carved deep scars into European history are well known, and stand today as a permanent reminder of the wickedness to which irrational bigotry, distorted religious conviction and religious intolerance, and racial hatreds can lead. What is less well known is that Poland's complex and often tortured history includes a long tradition of religious tolerance, betrayed by outbursts of Jewish persecution and, in some instances, enduring prejudice. The tradition of tolerance dates to at least the thirteenth century. Trade, immigration, and the country's ever-changing borders and fortunes tended to create an atmosphere more open to Jews than was common in other parts of the Christian world. That spirit of toleration led, early in Poland's history, to Jewish communities being granted rights of self-government.

In the aftermath of the Mongol sack of Kraków in 1241, many immigrants made their way to the royal city as it was rebuilt. Jews, frequently driven out of their homes in other European cities, found a welcome in the Polish capital as craftsmen, merchants, and financiers. While the Jewish community in Kraków was not without its struggles, the Jewish population was typically considered an important part of the city's cultural fabric, and tolerance was the rule more often than not. That tolerance was reciprocated by patriotism and Jewish loyalty to Poland. Thus in 1794, General Tadeusz Kościuszko, appealing to the Jewish community to aid the struggle for Polish independence, said: "The Jews proved to the world that whenever humanity can gain, they would not spare themselves." Kościuszko's testimony is memorialized on a plaque in the entrance hall of Kraków's **Great Synagogue.**

Kazimierz, the old Jewish district of Kraków, is bounded by

Great Synagogue, Kazimierz

ul. Starowiślna and ul. Krakowska; it was once an island surrounded by a tributary of the Vistula. The tributary has long
since been filled in, providing a connection between what was
once a separate town and the rest of Kraków; that geographic
reality was confirmed in law in 1791, when Kazimierz became
an administrative extension of the City of Kraków. The district's
name derives from its founding as a town by King Kazimierz the
Great, who in 1335 extended royal protection to the growing
Jewish community.

In the late fifteenth century, Jews who had lived near the
Academy of Kraków in the Old Town were forced to move to
Kazimierz to make room for an expanding campus. Over the
centuries, while Kazimierz became a major spiritual and cultural center of Polish Jewry, it was also a place for interethnic
and interreligious encounter, where different religious communities lived peaceably together.

With the coming of the Second World War, the Jews of Kazimierz were deported to a ghetto in the Podgorze district, just across the Vistula. The vast majority of the former residents of Kazimierz perished in the Holocaust, either in the ghetto or in the death camps.

The oldest extant synagogue in Poland, dating to the fifteenth century, is the **Great Synagogue** in Kazimierz, located at Szeroka 24. Also known as the Old Synagogue, the brick structure was first designed in a German and Bohemian Gothic style but was rebuilt after a 1577 fire according to Renaissance tastes by the Italian architect Mateo Gucci. In the sixteenth and seventeenth centuries, the synagogue included a vestibule, two prayer halls, and a building for community management. Later, all the buildings were combined into one complex, forming the religious-administrative center of the Jewish community in Kazimierz. The Great Synagogue's distinctive architectural features—high windows far above the ground, heavy buttressing, and stout walls—allowed it to serve as both fortress and temple, as frequent invasions of Kraków and occasional local persecutions made it necessary for the Jews of Kazimierz to have a place to protect themselves against siege.

Before and after World War I, in 1904, 1913, and 1923, the synagogue was renovated according to the architectural plans of Zygmunt Hendel.

The Great Synagogue of Kraków suffered virtually complete destruction during World War II. The Germans looted its artwork and religious artifacts; the complex was then taken over by the German Fiduciary Office (*Treuhandstelle*) and used as a munitions dump. In 1943, thirty Polish hostages were lined up against an exterior wall and shot; in 1944, the ceiling either collapsed or was intentionally destroyed.

The Great Synagogue was renovated between 1956 and 1959. It currently serves as a museum explaining the history and culture of Cracovian Jewry, and is part of the Historical Museum of Kraków. The museum is divided into two parts: the Main Hall displays the synagogue in as much of its original form as possible, along with features explaining the principal Jewish holidays, while the South Hall commemorates family and private life in the Cracovian Jewish community. The Main Hall features a Gothic ceiling with ribbed vaulting supported by long, slender columns, which date to the sixteenth century. In accordance with Jewish custom, the hall is almost bare; the only furnishing is the *bimah,* an elevated platform surrounded by an iron balustrade, from which the Torah was read. The east wall holds the *äron hakodesh,* a shrine encasing the Torah scrolls.

Memorial to murdered Hungarian Jews, KL-Płaszów

In 1978, the Great Synagogue was added to the list of UNESCO World Heritage Sites.

KL-Płaszów

The slave-labor or concentration camp, *Konzentrationslager Plaszow* in German, was built on the site of two Jewish cemeteries south of Kraków, shortly after the occupation began. Under its sadistic SS commandant Amon Göth, KL-Płaszów quickly became known for the extremities of its horrors, including the mass shooting of Jews and the torture of prisoners. After the liquidation of the ghetto from March 13–14, 1943, more than 8000 Jews thought to be fit to work were moved to Płaszów.

Today, the site's rolling hills and fields include a large stone memorial and several smaller monuments, including a memorial on the site where Göth personally executed prisoners.

The Schindler Factory/
"Kraków Under Occupation 1939–1945"

ul. Lipowa, 4

Many of the six thousand Cracovian Jews who survived the war were helped by Oskar Schindler, whose factory complex is now a museum commemorating and exploring various aspects of the occupation of Kraków from 1939 to 1945.

Oskar Schindler was born in 1908 in Moravia, now part of the Czech Republic, and started his career as an employee in his father's agricultural machinery factory. When the family firm closed because of the Great Depression, Schindler joined the Abwehr, the intelligence arm of the German armed forces, and shortly after became a member of Hitler's National Socialist German Workers Party.

When German troops arrived in Kraków on September 6, 1939, Schindler and his wife, Emilie, were ordered to the city, where Schindler took over, as trustee, a pot and pan shop as well as the Rekord factory, which made enameled products. Schindler built the two companies into a single, large operation, using capital from Jewish entrepreneurs in exchange for ready-made cookware products or employment. In 1943, Schindler finally became the legal owner of the company, *Deutsche Emailwarenfabrik* (German Enamel Works), or DEF.

While DEF continued to make enameled products, Schindler added a munitions department, which manufactured mess tins, cartridge cases, and fuses for artillery shells and bombs, an innovation that kept the company afloat financially.

In the early stages of DEF, Schindler employed mostly Poles, but by 1944, the number of Polish Jews working at the Schindler factory had grown from one hundred to almost eleven hundred. Prior to the 1943 liquidation of the Jewish ghetto in Podgórze, Jewish employees would be escorted to work from the ghetto. Those who survived the liquidation were moved to KL-Płaszów, a concentration camp. Schindler then built a subcamp of the Płaszów camp for his Jewish employees, and those of three nearby companies, on a lot he purchased adjacent to the DEF property in the Zabłocie district.

Schindler made considerable efforts to mitigate the harsh conditions in KL-Płaszów and at his factory. He reduced work shifts from twelve to eight hours, provided better food, and did what he could to temper the terrifying inspections by the sadistic Płaszów commandant, Amon Göth. In late 1944, as the Red Army rapidly approached Kraków, Schindler moved the staff and operations of DEF to Brünnlitz in Moravia. The factory continued production until the Soviets arrived in Czechoslovakia in May 1945.

When the war ended, Schindler and his wife received a letter from their Jewish employees, describing their humanitarian efforts, which eased the Schindlers' relocation to Germany. In 1963, Oskar Schindler was named one of the "Righteous Among the Nations" by the Yad Vashem Institute in Jerusalem. He died in 1974 in Hildesheim, Germany.

The Auschwitz-Birkenau Complex
Oświęcim

Oświęcim, some thirty-five miles from Kraków, is located in the part of Poland that was incorporated into the German Reich in 1939, when the town's name was changed to the German

Auschwitz I

Wall of Death, Auschwitz I

"Auschwitz." Because of its strategic location at the junction of numerous rail lines, Auschwitz and the surrounding area became the site of the most horrific of the German death camps, where well over a million innocent men, women, and children were exterminated in one of the world's first efforts at industrialized mass murder.

The first concentration camp in the area, known as Auschwitz I, was a former Polish army barracks transformed by the occupation into a labor camp for political prisoners. There, brutality reigned supreme: torture was common; unsuccessful escapees were hanged in public before the entire camp population; innumerable prisoners were shot at the Wall of Death, outside Block 11; a successful escape led to ten prisoners being chosen at random to die in the starvation bunker, Cell 18 of Block 11 (site of the martyrdom of St. Maximilian Kolbe). The

Auschwitz II–Birkenau

first experiments in mass execution in gas chambers, followed by cremation, took place at Auschwitz I, which eventually housed as many as fifteen thousand prisoners at a time.

The "Final Solution" to the "Jewish Question," outlined at the notorious Wannsee Conference in January 1942, required the acceleration, and thus industrialization, of mass murder—which led in turn to the designation of the Auschwitz II complex at Birkenau, the former Polish village of Brzezinka, located two miles from Auschwitz I, as a labor/extermination camp. Built to house some ninety thousand prisoners prior to their execution, Birkenau was the largest of the German death camps. St. Teresa Benedicta of the Cross (Edith Stein) was murdered at Birkenau in 1942, along with her sister, Rosa, their ashes scattered in a pond at the back of the complex.

Memorial, Auschwitz II–Birkenau

As the Red Army stormed toward Poland in January 1945, the perpetrators of the Holocaust tried to hide the evidence of their crimes by razing the Birkenau gas chambers and crematoria and destroying documents. Prisoners too weak to begin a forced march to Germany (along which many prisoners deemed fit soon died) were liberated by Soviet troops on January 27, 1945.

The many nations whose sons and daughters were slaughtered at what John Paul II called the "Golgotha of the modern world" are commemorated, country by country, at a stone and bronze memorial located at the end of the railroad tracks by which prisoners were transported, like cattle, to their deaths.

Auschwitz-Birkenau was added to the UNESCO World Heritage List in 1979. Today's state museum, headquartered at Auschwitz I, offers guided tours of many of the original camp structures. Permanent exhibits housed in the brick barracks of Auschwitz I explain the daily horrors of life in the camps and include poignant reminders of those who were slaughtered at Auschwitz, including seventy thousand infant shoes, thousands of prosthetic limbs, mounds of eyeglasses, and piles of shorn hair—all collected from those killed in the name of Nazi ideology.

On his first papal pilgrimage to Poland in June 1979, Pope John Paul II visited the Auschwitz-Birkenau complex, celebrated a Mass that included survivors of the camps, and prayed in the death cell of Maximilian Kolbe, where he left a Paschal candle that remains there today.

Contemporary Oświęcim is home to the Carmelite Convent of the Communion of Saints, located at Legionów 92a. [C.G.]

Pathways of a
Priest and Bishop

Wawel Cathedral

Wawel Cathedral with equestrian statue of Tadeusz Kościuszko

Wawel: The Royal Castle and Cathedral

Salvation History and World History

Wawel Hill is thick with history: political and religious history, made by kings, queens, courtiers, and bishops; cultural history, the creation of storytellers and musicians; the history of architecture and decoration, the work of architects, painters, weavers, and sculptors; the personal histories, replete with triumph and tragedy, of those who lived here, are buried here, or have made pilgrimage here. To stand on Wawel is to be immersed in a millennium of history. But what is this "history" that can be touched and seen and felt here? The remarkably rich historical texture of this epicenter of Polish national identity invites a reflection on the relationship between world history and salvation history, between "history" as it is understood by historians and journalists and "history" understood as what philosopher Peter Kreeft calls "His-story": the story of the God of the Bible at work in the world.

Insofar as the late modern and postmodern world thinks of "spirituality," it tends to imagine the life of the spirit as the human quest for the transcendent, the divine, the Other. That is not, however, how biblical religion thinks of the spiritual life. Biblical religion is not about the human search for God. Biblical religion is about God's search for us: the God of the Bible comes into history and asks his people—first, the People of Israel, later, the people of the Church—to take the same path into the future that God is taking. That is the bright thread that weaves Exodus and the Gospels, the Prophets and St. Paul, into a single tapestry of revelation: God taking the lead and, as it were, clearing the path, with the people of God learning, often the hard way, to follow that path.

Read through biblical lenses, then, "history" really is "History." And that brings world history, as it is (or used to be) taught in elementary and secondary schools, into a new light.

Until recently, "world history" was taught to youngsters in a linear fashion, under chapter headings that divided "world history" into manageable chunks, one following the other: Early Civilizations, Greece and Rome, the Dark Ages, the Middle Ages, Renaissance and Reformation, the Age of Science, the Age of Revolution, the Space Age. There's obviously truth here; that is more or less how the history of the world has unfolded (at least viewed from the perspective of the West). But from a biblical point of view, to "read" world history through those conventional chapter headings is to remain on the surface of history, seeing only what might be recorded by an ancient chronicler or poet, or a modern reporter.

The biblical view of history—history as God's search for humanity, and our learning to take the same road through history that God is taking—suggests a different set of chapter headings for a true world history: Creation, Fall, Promise, Prophecy, Incarnation, Redemption, Sanctification, the

Kingdom of God. Reading world history through lenses ground by biblical faith, according to those chapter headings, allows us to "see" history in its true depth and against its most ample horizon. Reading history as "His-story" gets things into proper—and breathtaking—perspective. For, read as His-story, history comes into focus as the history of salvation: a history that begins not with randomness but with purpose; a history that ends not with oblivion but with a great, cosmic, eternal party, the Wedding Feast of the Lamb, described in the twenty-first chapter of the Book of Revelation.

Moreover, in the biblical view of things (which is how Karol Wojtyła, St. John Paul II, looked at things), salvation history and world history do not unfold on parallel tracks, as if world history is *here* and salvation history is *there*. No, salvation history *is* world history, read truly. Salvation history is the depth dimension of world history. Salvation history is what is happening *inside* world history, whether the world recognizes that dynamic within itself or not. Salvation history is what is drawing history on, not mechanically but spiritually.

UNDERSTANDING THE TRUTH of biblical religion as the drama of God's search for us is important in itself, because it is an antidote to that great deadener of perceptions, boredom. Living history, including our individual personal histories, as our participation in His-story is endless adventure—and adventure is never boring. Understanding history as God's salvific search for us is also important in meeting the challenge of what the great twentieth-century French theologian Henri de Lubac called "atheistic humanism," which has been a destructive dynamic in Western civilization for more than two centuries now.

Atheists—those who are, literally, *a-Theos,* "without God" or "without the gods"—are nothing new. What was new in nineteenth-century Europe, de Lubac argued, was an atheism that condemned the God of the Bible as the enemy of human liberation and maturation—the God who must be cast aside if humanity were to grow up and live in freedom. This, de Lubac suggested, was turning things upside down in a great, and potentially harmful, inversion. For the God of the Bible had come into history as a liberator, and to miss that truth was to miss something essential to the civilization of the West.

Ancient gods were fearsome deities. The Philistine god Moloch demanded, and got, the sacrifice of children, against which the prophets of Israel railed as against no other form of wickedness. The Aztec deities of ancient Mexico were thought to be appeased by the vivisection of those offered to them in sacrifice, their beating hearts ripped out at the summit of great sacrificial pyramids. Then there were the Greek gods: a bit more humane, perhaps, but whimsical on some occasions, cruel on others, deities for whom even the strongest of humans (think of Achilles in the *Iliad*) were, in the final analysis, playthings on a cosmic game board. Into *that* kind of spiritual cosmos, the God of the Bible—the God of Abraham and Moses, the God whom Jesus called "Father"—came as a liberator.

The God of the Bible did not demand human sacrifice; the God of the Bible condemned this ancient abomination. The God of the Bible did not play games with his creation; the God of the Bible freed his people from slavery, both chattel slavery and the slavery of sin. The God of the Bible did not leave men and women in confusion or fear about their lives and their futures; the God of the Bible created humanity with an instinct for goodness, gave his people a moral code to prevent them from falling back into the habits of the slaves they had been, and offered them a future in which the consummation of history would be not a conflagration but the satisfaction of the deepest desires of the human heart.

That God is a liberator, and it is a calumny to suggest otherwise. To understand history as His-story armors twenty-first-century men and women against that calumny, even as it reveals the shallowness, indeed the silliness, of the "New Atheists" and their project.

TO UNDERSTAND THAT salvation history is the deep current running inside world history is also to understand, with St. John Paul II, that life has an inherently *dramatic* structure.

Karol Wojtyła's theatrical experience gave him a useful set of skills. Sir John Gielgud, a superb actor in his own right, once commented on John Paul II's remarkable sense of timing in his public addresses. Another great figure of the twentieth-century stage, Sir Alec Guinness (a distinguished Shakespearean long before he became known as Obi-Wan Kenobi), wrote in his diaries of John Paul II's strikingly clear voice—a way of articulating things in public that he began to learn from Mieczysław Kotlarcyzk and which he practiced at length with his fellow members of the Rhapsodic Theater.

Yet Wojtyła's immersion in the theater, which included his experience as a playwright, was more than a matter of acquiring a set of skills; it shaped both his mind and the dramatic layer of his soul. It was a matter of acquiring a worldview, a way of seeing things that complemented both his biblical view of the world as the arena of salvation history and his philosophical reflections on human moral agency.

And in that way of looking at things, every human person lives inside a drama. Each of us lives, every day, in the gap between the person I am and the person I ought to be—which is an inherently dramatic situation. "Mind the gap" is a ubiquitous safety instruction on the London Underground, reminding Tube passengers not to get their feet caught between the train and the platform edge. "Mind the gap" is also, however, a very good description of the moral drama of the human condition. To "mind the gap" is to be mindful, daily, that life is journey and pilgrimage, and that we become better-fitted for following the trail that God is blazing through history when, by cooperating with God's grace, we try to close the gap between the person I am and the person I ought to be.

Wojtyła's biblical faith taught him something more about the dramatic character of the human condition: it taught him that each of our personal dramas "plays" within a cosmic and historical drama, the drama of salvation history. And that drama has God as producer, director, scriptwriter—and, ultimately, protagonist, for God himself enters the drama fully, in the person of his Son, so that the drama of history might be redirected to its proper trajectory, which leads from the creation to the Wedding Feast of the Lamb. Thus we do not live our personal dramas by ourselves. We are, as the Letter to the Hebrews teaches, surrounded by a "great cloud of witnesses" (Hebrews 12:1), who, alongside us and before us and ahead of us, are living, or have lived, the drama of their lives within the great drama of salvation history.

WE ARE NOT, then, alone. There is company on the road. The Creed calls that company the "Communion of Saints," and it, too, is palpable on Wawel Hill. For as the Catholic Church understands the Communion of Saints, it includes those who have gone before us and now rest in God (the Church Triumphant); those who are being purified in Purgatory so that they can rest at ease in God (the Church Suffering); and those who are still *in via*, on the way (the Church Militant). The "cloud of witnesses" surrounding each of us and the drama of our individual lives is incalculably, indeed incomprehensibly, vast; but in a place like Wawel, we can touch, at least imaginatively, the extraordinary diversity of witnesses whose personal dramas can inspire us to "mind the gap" more faithfully along our own pilgrimage.

The obvious and primary witnesses atop Wawel are the canonized saints: Stanisław and Jadwiga, whose relics have been venerated here for centuries by millions, and John Paul II, whose relics are now venerated here as well. But the cloud of witnesses at Wawel is not composed only of canonized saints. It includes great figures who left a decisive imprint on history. Here is King Jan III Sobieski, victor at the Battle of Vienna in 1683, which made the Europe we know today possible. Here is General Tadeusz Kościuszko, who fought for liberty under the banner "For Your Freedom and Ours," and who was more successful in aiding the cause of American independence than in securing Poland's liberties. And here is

Tomb of St. Jadwiga,
Wawel Cathedral

General Władysław Sikorski, the embodiment of "Fighting Poland" during the darkest days of World War II.

Their presence here, entombed close by the canonized saints, prompts another reflection: What makes a place holy? Is it the relics venerated at a place such as Wawel Cathedral? Those relics reflect Catholicism's incarnational imagination, the Catholic conviction that "stuff counts," and that the human body has an innate dignity, even sanctity, conferred by the fact that we are ultimately the creation of God and that the Son of God took on our flesh, thus ennobling it in a unique way among the things of creation. But relics are not all there is in the making of holy places.

Shrines such as Wawel are made holy by the grace of God at work in the cloud of witnesses who come to pray in these places. Hundreds of years of prayer have sanctified places such as Wawel Cathedral, including the prayers offered in thanksgiving for the lives of those all too human and fallible great figures of history who are buried here. They, too, lived "in the gap," and struggled to narrow it, some more successfully than others. Prayers of thanksgiving for their lives and for the happy repose of their souls sanctify their tombs, and places such as Wawel, because those prayers arise in response to God's thirst for us, which is the wellspring of all prayer:

> Then came a woman of Samaria to draw water. Jesus said to her, "Give me a drink." ... The Samaritan woman said to him, "How is it that you, a Jew, ask a drink of me, a woman of Samaria?" ... Jesus said to her, "If you knew the gift of God, and who it is that is saying to you, 'Give me a drink,' you would have asked him, and he would have given you living water." [John 4:7, 9–10]

Prayer, the work of God within us, makes shrines holy.

WAWEL CATHEDRAL WAS the seat of Karol Wojtyła's ministry as archbishop of Kraków from 1964 to 1978; his life forms a bridge between this holy place and another great basilica, St. Peter's in Rome, itself sanctified by the relics of the Passion and of the saints, and by the prayers of untold millions of Christians. In the drama of Wojtyła's life, however, Wawel holds a special place of honor. Here he was serving Mass on September 1, 1939, when World War II began and German bombs fell on Kraków; here he was ordained a bishop, and

later received by the Cathedral Chapter as metropolitan archbishop and cardinal. Above all, this is where he chose to celebrate his first Masses as a priest, on November 2, 1946.

He had been ordained the day before, in the chapel at the
episcopal residence, by Cardinal Adam Stefan Sapieha, the
"unbroken prince" who had stood fast against Nazi tyranny
during the long, dark night of occupation. Now it was his moment to celebrate the sacred mysteries for the first time—and
because tradition allowed priests to celebrate three Masses on
behalf of the dead on All Souls Day, to repeat that first Mass
twice more. As he tells us in his vocational memoir, *Gift and
Mystery,* he chose the **St. Leonard Crypt** of Wawel Cathedral
for these three "first Masses" in order to "express my special
spiritual bond with the history of Poland" and to pay tribute to the panoply of Polish heroes buried nearby, "who were
extremely influential in my education as a Christian and a

St. Leonard Crypt, Wawel Cathedral

patriot." It was the decision of a radically converted Christian deeply imbued with the Catholic incarnational imagination. History is His-story. The great figures of history lived out the drama of their individual lives and struggles inside salvation history, in which the God of the Bible is always at work, even in mysterious ways. That was the conviction that led Father Karol Wojtyła to St. Leonard's Crypt in Wawel Cathedral on November 2, 1946. That was the conviction in which he wrote by hand, on the holy cards commemorating his ordination, a line from Mary's Magnificat: *Fecit mihi magna* (He has done great things for me).

Wawel

Wawel, the "Polish Zion," is a limestone hill overlooking a bend in the Vistula on the river's left bank, immediately south of and adjacent to Kraków's Old Town. Home to the **Royal Castle** and the **Cathedral of St. Stanisław and St. Wenceslaus,** Wawel is the heart of the city, and indeed of all Poland: a complex of venerable structures that combines elements of Westminster Abbey and Buckingham Palace, the White House and Arlington National Cemetery, in a singularly rich history.

While legend attributes the city's origins to the mythical prince Krak, who defeated a dragon that terrorized the local maidens from his Wawel cave, Kraków's eminence as the repository of Polish national identity can be traced to King Kazimierz I Odnowiciel ("the Restorer"), great-grandson of the Piast prince Mieszko I, whose conversion to Christianity in 966 set what would become Poland on its unique historical course. It was

Kazimierz the Restorer (whose rule spanned two decades, from 1034 until 1058) who, against the competing claims of Gzniezo and Poznań, firmly centered royal authority and thus Polish political power in Kraków, where it remained for more than five centuries.

Gniezno, one of many claimants to be the site of the baptism of Mieszko, remained the country's spiritual center, however, until the early fourteenth century, when Wawel and its cathedral became a major pilgrimage site to which pilgrims flocked in order to venerate the relics of a local bishop, Stanisław of Szczepanów, martyred at the hands of King Bolesław II Szczodry ("the Bold") in 1079; the bishop was canonized by Pope Innocent IV in 1253. The cult of St. Stanisław led Polish kings, eager to demonstrate their devotion to a national saint martyred by one of their predecessors, to be crowned in Wawel Cathedral. The coronation of King Władysław I Łokietek ("the Short") in 1320 was the first such ceremony conducted in the cathedral, and the tradition continued for more than four centuries.

During the city's golden age, from the mid-fifteenth through the late sixteenth century, Kraków reached the apex of its influence and the Wawel court, centered on the Royal Castle, rivaled others throughout Europe for splendor, hosting nobility from all over the continent. In 1517, King Zygmunt I Stary ("the Old") married the Italian noblewoman Bona Sforza (daughter of the duke of Milan, cousin of the king of France, and niece of the wife of the Holy Roman Emperor), who brought the best of Italian Renaissance architecture and art to Kraków, much of it fashioned by the leading Italian artisans of the day. Traces of that period of Cracovian history can be found in the Italian-based words that continue to be sprinkled throughout the Polish language, including "pomidor" (from the Italian *pomodoro*, or tomato), "arancio" (*arancia*, orange), and "scarpetta" (in Polish, "sock," and in Italian, "little shoe").

The transfer of the Polish capital to Warsaw in 1596 inevitably led to a decline in Wawel's fortunes. In addition to the depredations caused by disease, famine, and fires, the seventeenth and eighteenth centuries were marked by continual eruptions of the Polish tendency to indulge in political infighting and intrigue, which, combined with the rapaciousness of the neighboring great powers, eventually resulted in the Polish partitions of 1772, 1793, and 1795. The Third Partition completed the destruction of independent Poland, as its remaining territory was absorbed by Russia, Prussia, and Austria, and Kraków became a city in Austrian Galicia.

Yet during the 123 years when "Poland" was lost to the map of Europe, Wawel experienced something of a revival. The Royal Castle was a reminder of past glories. More important, the cathedral's crypts held the remains of centuries of Polish monarchs and other national heroes, in addition to the relics of St. Stanisław and Queen Jadwiga, the latter venerated in a popular cult since her death in 1399. Thus Wawel became a unique repository of Poland's national identity and a pilgrimage site for generations of Poles yearning for the recovery of their national independence.

The fabric of the Royal Castle and Wawel Cathedral suffered relatively little damage during the Nazi occupation; the castle was the residence of the governor-general of the *General Gouvernement*, Hans Frank (later executed at Nuremberg as a war criminal). Just prior to the outbreak of World War II, many of the castle's precious historical treasures were removed as a precaution against German looting; some were hidden as far away as Canada and were returned in the decades after the war.

The Royal Castle

Although kings lived on Wawel from the early centuries of the second millennium, very little of today's Royal Castle is older than the fourteenth century. Kazimierz the Great's room is the principal structure remaining from that period; it contains a late fourteenth-century fresco with Queen Jadwiga's monogram.

Today's castle is very much the product of the sixteenth and seventeenth centuries, when the Polish monarchy was strongly influenced by the Italian Renaissance, an influence strengthened by the marriage of King Zygmunt I Stary (who reigned from 1505 to 1548) to Bona Sforza. Tearing down the old Gothic structures, Zygmunt had a Renaissance palace built by the Florentine architect Bartolommeo Berrecci; completed in 1540, it featured stately halls and an extensive courtyard surrounded by arcaded galleries. His successor, Zygmunt II August (who reigned from 1548 to 1572), imported a magnificent collection of Flemish tapestries to enhance and warm the castle's interior; many of them survive today.

Thanks to its location on a hill, the Royal Castle and the adjacent cathedral were spared many of the devastating fires that befell Kraków. The castle did, however, suffer its own fires. After a 1595 conflagration that only left the Senatorial Room (home to many of the prized Flemish tapestries) unscathed, Zygmunt III Vasa (who reigned from 1587 to 1632) hired Italian artisans, including architect Giovanni Trevano and painter Tomasso Dolabella, to rebuild the palace.

Today, castle tours include the State Rooms, the Royal Private Apartments, the guest apartments, the suite for the governor of Kraków, the Treasury and Armory, a permanent archaeological exhibit, and temporary exhibits. The coffered ceilings in the Envoys' Rooms feature unique woodcarvings of thirty human heads, in addition to the castle's priceless sixteenth-century Flemish tapestries. The Sigismund Tower contains a large collection of portraits of Polish kings and other royalty, as well as numerous historical paintings, many of them from the Dutch school. The Treasury and Armory have an exceptional array of artifacts collected over the centuries, despite the numerous raids made upon the Royal Castle's treasures by invading armies and looting marauders. The collection includes medieval suits of armor, crowns, scepters, and the castle's most prized possession: the *Szczerbiec,* the sword used in most royal coronations from 1320–1764.

The Cathedral of St. Stanisław and St. Wenceslaus

The metropolitan cathedral of Kraków, now raised to the dignity of a basilica, is the most important church in Poland. Here, in addition to the remains of centuries of monarchs and national heroes, Poles can venerate the relics of two of the nation's patron saints, the martyred bishop, Stanisław, and the virtuous queen, Jadwiga (canonized on the **Błonia Krakowskie** by John Paul II in 1997), as well as a relic of St. John Paul II himself.

The first cathedral church was likely built shortly after Kraków was established as a diocese in 1000, and though little is known about the actual structure, it was likely of Romanesque design. A second Romanesque cathedral was begun

Tomb of St. Stanisław,
Wawel Cathedral

by King Bolesław II (who reigned from 1058 to 1079) but
was finished by his successors when the king was forced to
flee Poland after the murder of Bishop Stanisław. The triple-
aisle cathedral, constructed of limestone and sandstone, was
consecrated in 1142. Remnants of that structure include St.
Leonard's Crypt, site of Fr. Karol Wojtyła's first Masses on All
Souls Day, 1946, at an altar then framed by the stone sarcoph-
agi of General Tadeusz Kościuszko, Prince Józef Poniatowski,
King Jan III Sobieski and his wife, Maria Kazimiera, and King
Michał Korybut Wiśnowiecki; the stone sarcophagus of General Władysław Sikorski was added to the crypt after the fall of
Polish communism.

As age and fire took their toll on the Romanesque church, a Gothic cathedral was built in its place. Begun with the presbytery, completed in 1346, the triple-aisled structure was consecrated on March 28, 1364. During the remainder of the fourteenth century and throughout the fifteenth, several side chapels were constructed along the external walls of the church, many as crypts for noble families.

The sixteenth century brought the influence of the Italian Renaissance to Wawel Cathedral. Built between 1515 and 1533, King Zygmunt I's Royal Chapel was the monarch's mausoleum; known today as the Sigismund Chapel, it is considered one of the finest extant examples of High Renaissance architecture. Designed by the Florentine Bartolommeo Berrecci, the architect for the renovated castle, it served as a model for other Renaissance and mannerist mausoleums throughout the cathedral. King Zygmunt also commissioned the enormous bell, named the Sigismund Bell, which is the largest of the five cathedral bells. As it weighs almost twenty-eight thousand pounds, twelve bellmen are required to ring it, a feat that marks the most important national occasions.

During the seventeenth and eighteenth centuries, the majority of the cathedral's interior furnishings were replaced with baroque and late baroque paintings, stalls, and altars, the last using black- and rose-colored marbles from Polish quarries; most of the baroque designs were created or executed by Italian artists or Poles trained in Italy. The city's bishops were buried in various parts of the cathedral; among the most notable from recent decades are Cardinal Jan Puzyna, the last elector to cast a political veto in a papal conclave, who is buried in today's St. John Paul II Chapel, and Cardinal Adam Stefan Sapieha, the heroic archbishop of the occupation, who is buried in front of the silver coffin of St. Stanisław in the cathedral's nave.

In addition to celebrating his first Masses in St. Leonard's Crypt on November 2, 1946, Karol Wojtyła was ordained a bishop in Wawel Cathedral on September 28, 1958 (the liturgical memorial of St. Wenceslaus, one of the cathedral's patrons), and was enthroned in Wawel's episcopal *cathedra* as the seventy-sixth archbishop of Kraków on March 8, 1964. As pope, John Paul II visited Wawel Cathedral in 1979, 1983, 1987, 1991, 1997, 1999, and 2002.

The Cathedral Museum

Located across a small courtyard from the entrance to Wawel Cathedral, the Cathedral Museum is located in Cathedral House, itself composed of a pair of fourteenth-century buildings. Originally called the Diocesan Museum, it was established in 1906. In 1975, Cardinal Karol Wojtyła decided to transform it into the Cathedral Museum, where objects from the Wawel Cathedral would be kept and displayed. The cardinal opened and blessed the new museum on September 28, 1978, the twentieth anniversary of his ordination as a bishop in Wawel Cathedral—his last official ceremony at Wawel before his election as pope on October 16, 1978. Shortly thereafter, the Cathedral Chapter added the Polish pope's name to the Cathedral Museum; a bronze statue of John Paul II was erected in front of the museum in 2008.

The Cathedral Museum exhibits feature the most precious objects from the Cathedral treasury, including Polish royal regalia, noteworthy paintings and sculptures, and memorabilia from John Paul II's years as archbishop.

The Dean's House and the Archdiocesan Museum
ul. Kanonicza, 19–21

These two adjacent townhouses, now interconnected, were Karol Wojtyła's home from 1951 (when he moved to Kanonicza 21 from St. Florian's in order to work on his *habilitation* thesis) until 1967 (when, after renovations to the Metropolitan Curia, he left Kanonicza 19, where he had lived for some years, and took up residence in the archbishop's traditional home).

The **"Dean's House"** at Kanonicza 21 was the traditional home of the dean of the Chapter of Wawel Cathedral, a senior group of priests with responsibilities for both the cathedral and the archdiocese. Nestled at the base of Wawel Hill, the Dean's House is one of the best-preserved historic houses in the city.

Dean's House (Kanonicza 21)

The original fourteenth-century home was remodeled over a decade in the late sixteenth century, when the Italian architect Santi Gucci transformed the original Gothic structure into a mannerist residence with an arcaded interior courtyard. Today, the late Renaissance portal still bears the inscription *Procul este profani* (Stay away, profane ones).

The Dean's House was transformed from an active residence into the Archdiocesan Museum of Kraków in 1994. Today, visitors to the museum can see the lodgings of its most famous resident, along with many of his personal belongings, such as his professor's gown, bishop's and cardinal's cassocks, manuscripts, published books, fountain pens, a pair of skis, and a kayak, as well as artifacts from John Paul's pontificate including photographs, medals, paintings, vestments, rosaries, and chalices. [C.G.]

Skałka

Religious Freedom, the First of Human Rights

In a conversation with members of Congress in the early 1980s, the distinguished British historian Michael Howard, who would go on to occupy the Regius Professorship of

Basilica of St. Michael and St. Stanisław

Modern History at Oxford and be knighted, remarked that there had been two great twentieth-century revolutions. The first, he said, began in 1917, when Lenin's Bolsheviks expropriated the Russian people's revolution, overthrew Russia's nascent constitutional monarchy, and launched the world's first totalitarian experiment. The second, he mused, was under way even as he spoke: the transformation of the Catholic Church from a defender of the *ancien régime* and established political power into the world's foremost institutional defender of human rights. Little did Michael Howard know that, less than a decade later, the second twentieth-century revolution, the Catholic human rights revolution, would play a significant role in the collapse of the communist regimes in central and eastern Europe: regimes created by the heirs of the first great twentieth-century revolution, the Bolshevik revolution.

AT THE CENTER of the Catholic human rights revolution stood Pope John Paul II, the man who focused more than a century of Catholic social thought about the morally appropriate ways to organize modern political communities through the clarifying prism of basic human rights. And at the center of John Paul II's defense and promotion of human rights was his insistence that religious freedom was the first of civil and political rights. That was another lesson the Polish pope brought from Kraków to the world, a lesson whose roots can be traced here to Skałka and to the central place of St. Stanisław, the martyr bishop of Kraków, in the tradition of the bishops of Kraków and their role as *defensor civitatis*—the "defender of the city," its people, and their rights.

Almost a century before the death of St. Thomas Becket in Canterbury, Stanisław was murdered at Skałka by King Bolesław the Bold, who thought the bishop a danger to his authority. Whatever the precise details of their dispute may have been, the devotion to the martyred bishop that quickly developed in Kraków, the miraculous cures attributed to his intercession, and the emergence of the site of his martyrdom and his tomb as a major pilgrimage shrine drove home a message that would resonate down the centuries: Stanisław died in defense of the *libertas ecclesiae,* the freedom of the Church, and in doing so, he died in defense of the moral truth that arbitrary and despotic state power is unjust state power, a threat to the lives and liberties of the people.

His twentieth-century successors in the bishop's chair of Kraków took up the mantle of *defensor civitatis* against two totalitarian systems, Nazism and communism, adding their own heroic chapters to the story of the Cracovian episcopate. During the dark night of the occupation, Archbishop Adam Stefan Sapieha became the living symbol of Poland's refusal to be erased, as the Nazis intended. St. Stanisław, one suspects, would have approved of Sapieha's style. After months of being badgered for a dinner invitation by Hans Frank, the head of Gestapoland (more formally known as the *General Gouvernement*), Sapieha issued the invitation to the credibility-seeking Nazi overlord—and then served him a meal consisting of black bread (made in part from acorns), beet jam, and ersatz coffee. When Frank stared down the table at his aristocratic host, Sapieha blandly explained that this was the diet on which his people were expected to live, according to the food coupons available from the occupation, and the archbishop of Kraków certainly couldn't risk the arrest of one of his servants by dealing on the black market in order to feed the governor. Not for nothing was Sapieha known, during the war, as "the uncrowned king of Poland."

Sapieha's successor, Eugeniusz Baziak, was a determined foe of the new "occupying power," the Polish Communist Party, during some of the worst years of Polish Stalinism: a man who subordinated his own natural warmth and capacity for friendship to the imperative of maintaining a facade of stern and inflexible resistance to the communist usurpation of Poland's liberties. Denied the title "Archbishop of Kraków" by the Polish communist authorities, who refused to accept his appointment by Pope Pius XII, he died in 1962—and was buried beneath a tombstone in Wawel Cathedral on which the people of Kraków inscribed the title the communists refused him. Then, after Cardinal Karol Wojtyła vigorously defended the human rights of all during two years as apostolic administrator and twelve years as archbishop of Kraków, his successor, Cardinal Franciszek Macharski, assumed the ancient role of *defensor civitatis*. When martial law was declared in Poland in December 1981, Macharski demanded the release of those detained without trial in prison camps or under house arrest, visited prisoners, and served as a clandestine conduit between the imprisoned leaders of the Solidarity movement and their families—and between the Solidarity leadership and the Polish pope in Rome.

THE STANISŁAW TRADITION has been developed over the centuries by some striking personalities, to be sure. The ultimate foundation of this heroic exercise of the priesthood and the episcopate is not personal, however, but sacramental. According to Catholic theology, Holy Orders sacramentally configures a man to Christ the Good Shepherd in a unique way and calls the ordinand to an ongoing exercise of pastoral charity—the distinctive way in which celibate Catholic priests and bishops exercise paternity. Holy Orders, in turn, rests upon the foundation of what Catholicism knows as the *sacraments of initiation:* Baptism, Confirmation, and the Holy Eucharist. A man must first be a fully initiated disciple of the Lord Jesus Christ before he can be an icon of Christ the Good Shepherd as priest or bishop. Thus at Skałka the new **Altar of the Three Millennia**—which honors five native-born Polish saints, an adoptive Polish saint, and the heroic prior of the monastery of the Black Madonna when it was besieged by the Swedes in 1655—includes a steel monolith celebrating these first sacraments, with saintly Polish priests and bishops depicted baptizing, confirming, and distributing Holy Communion.

THUS ONE ROOT of the contemporary Catholic human rights revolution, and its emphasis on religious freedom as the first of civil and political rights, reaches back to Skałka. And that prompts, in this historic place, a reflection on what "religious freedom" means.

Religious conviction creates religious communities; those communities express the convictions that make them what they are in various ways. One such expression is worship, and freedom to worship is surely one component of religious freedom.

Monolith of the sacraments of initiation, Altar of the Three Millennia

But it is not the only dimension of the first freedom, the claims of some twenty-first-century governments notwithstanding. Religious communities conduct educational, health care, and charitable institutions, provide social services, sponsor publications, and take their part in the debates of public life—all as expressions of their religious convictions. To deny that the protections of religious freedom apply to these institutions and activities is to reduce religious freedom to a personal lifestyle choice. Poland's communist authorities would likely have been delighted to "respect" the religious freedom of Polish Catholics had Polish Catholicism been willing to redefine religious freedom as simply freedom of worship. That Polish Catholics and their leaders were unwilling to do so—that Poland's Catholics insisted on their right, as believers, to build churches, conduct schools, form youth groups, run newspapers and magazines, provide nursing and other health care services, train their clergy according to the Church's standards, and, in general, manage their own religious affairs without state interference—was a bold witness to religious freedom in full that eventually won out over coercive and despotic state power.

The modern state, in its various forms, seems to have an insatiable impulse to expand the scope of its authority and the reach of its administrative power. Poland's communists did this in a dramatic way when, in 1953, the communist government attempted to implement a law on Church appointments by which state authorities, not Church authorities, would appoint and remove bishops, pastors, and assistant pastors— thus making the Polish Church a de facto department of the Polish communist state. Meeting in Kraków, under the leadership of the heroic Cardinal Stefan Wyszyński and in the shadow of St. Stanisław and Skałka, the bishops of Poland boldly and unhesitatingly followed the Stanisław tradition. In a dramatic statement, the bishops condemned the communist government's "radical, destructive hatred towards Catholicism," called on the state to abandon "its aim of subjugating the Church and turning it into an instrument of the State," and then, in a final, concluding gesture of defiance, said, "We are not allowed to place the things of God on the altar of Caesar. *Non possumus!* [We cannot!]"

In the Western world of the early twenty-first century, encroachments on religious freedom tend to be more subtle. But when the bishops of the United States were confronted in 2011 with what they regarded as a frontal assault on religious freedom by an American government determined to compel Catholic institutions to include contraceptives and abortifacients in the health care insurance they provided their employees, the bishops (many of whom were quite aware of the 1953 Polish example), drew a line in the sand and challenged the government in court—not only in the name of Catholic institutions, but also for the sake of conscientious Catholic employers who did not want the health insurance they included in their employees' benefits to include "reproductive health services" the Church considered immoral. Similar pressures have been put on other Christians in the early twenty-first century, in a variety of ways. A Canadian evangelical pastor was fined a considerable amount of money by a provincial "human rights tribunal" in Alberta for what the politically correct deemed "hate speech"—the pastor in question had preached in support of the biblical understanding of marriage, in his own church.

These assaults on religious freedom do not, of course, begin to compare with the pressures—often lethal pressures—put on Christians in majority-Islamic states or regions in which radical Islamist or jihadist forces have assumed political power. Christians are the most persecuted religious group in the early twenty-first-century world, and that persecution is largely, although not exclusively, at the hands of radical

Islamists and jihadists. This twenty-first-century persecution, in turn, comes hard on the heels of the greatest century of persecution in Christian history. According to the Commission on New Martyrs created by Pope John Paul II in preparation for the Great Jubilee of 2000, far more Christians were killed in hatred of the faith in the twentieth century than in the previous nineteen centuries of Christian history combined. Yet this omnipresence of martyrdom in the life of the contemporary Church barely registers on the consciousness of most Catholics in the West.

All the more reason, then, to come to Skałka, to reflect on the cost of discipleship, to take courage from those such as St. Stanisław who have borne faithful witness in the past, and to recommit oneself to the defense of the religious freedom of all in the future.

Altar of St. Stanisław
with John Paul II votum,
Basilica of St. Michael
and St. Stanisław

SUCH A COMMITMENT requires ongoing and deepening conversion to Christ, and to the truths that Christ embodies. John Paul II preached about that to young people during his first pastoral pilgrimage to Poland in June 1979, evoking the memory of St. Stanisław and Skałka:

> When we listen to the Gospel that the liturgy of the solemnity of Saint Stanisław each year recalls to us, we see in our mind's eye Christ, the Good Shepherd who "lays down his life for the sheep" (John 10:11), who knows his own sheep and his own know him (cf. John 10:14), who goes after the lost sheep and, when he has

St. Stanisław; Altar of the Three Millennia

found it, "he lays it on his shoulders, rejoicing" (Luke 15:5), and brings it back with joy to the fold.

All that I can say to you is summed up in the words: Get to know Christ and make yourselves known to him. He knows each one of you in a particular way. It is not a knowledge that arouses opposition and rebellion, a knowledge that forces one to flee in order to safeguard his own inward mystery. It is not a knowledge made up of hypotheses and reducing man to his dimensions of social utility. The knowledge of Christ is a knowledge full of the simple truth about "man" and, above all, full of love. Submit yourselves to this simple and loving knowledge of the Good Shepherd. Be certain that he knows each one of you more than each one of you knows himself. He knows because he has laid down his life (cf. John 15:13).

Allow him to find you. A human being, a young person, at times gets lost in himself, in the world about him, and in all the network of human affairs that wrap him round. Allow Christ to find you. Let him know all about you and guide you. It is true that following someone requires also making demands on our selves. That is the law of friendship. If we wish to travel together, we must pay attention to the road we are to take. If we go walking in the mountains, we must follow the signs. If we go mountain climbing, we cannot let go of the rope. We must also preserve our unity with the Divine Friend whose name is Jesus Christ. We must cooperate with him.

Remember [that what] I . . . am saying now . . . I am saying . . . from personal experience. I have always been amazed at the wonderful power that Christ holds over the human heart: he holds it not for just any reason or motive, not for any kind of career or profit, but only because he loves and lays down his life for his brethren (cf. John 15:13).

Then, having called the young people of Kraków and Poland to conversion, he called them to mission, to fearlessness, and to their Catholic and public duty:

You are the future of the world, of the nation, of the Church. "Tomorrow depends on you." Accept with a sense of responsibility the simple truth contained in this song of youth and ask Christ, through his Mother, that you may be able to face it.

You must carry into the future the whole of the experience of history that is called "Poland." It is a difficult experience, perhaps one of the most difficult in the world, in Europe, and in the Church. Do not be afraid of the toil; be afraid only of thoughtlessness and pusillanimity. From the difficult experience that we call "Poland" a better future can be drawn, but only on condition that you are honorable, temperate, believing, free in spirit, and strong in your convictions.

Skałka

The powerful hold that St. Stanisław exerts on Poland's self-understanding as a symbol of national unity and religious freedom reflects the country's volatile political history: a history often plagued by divisiveness among the Polish gentry and nobility, which made the country vulnerable time and again to foreign invasion and exploitation.

The Polish gentry class (the *Szlachta,* in Polish) was the largest in percentage terms in Europe; some 8 to 10 percent of the population claimed noble status, compared with 2–3 percent of the population elsewhere. This large and often unruly class of gentry, all of whom asserted a right to membership in the parliament, the *Sejm* (where matters had to be decided unanimously), was a significant check on royal power—and a considerable factor in governmental paralysis. Moreover, from the mid-sixteenth century on, the Polish monarchy was elective, and kings were dependent throughout their reigns on the coalitions of gentry they had assembled to secure their election. Thus Polish history is rife with crises of authority, which too often coincided with foreign pressures and intrigues—all of which eventually resulted in the three partitions of Poland that took place in the eighteenth century and the end of Polish independence in 1795.

Throughout this tumultuous history, Poland could look to its first native saint as a symbol of the hope for a greater measure of national unity—and could do so because of the traditions surrounding that saint's martyrdom and the miraculous reconstitution of his divided remains.

The Basilica of St. Michael and St. Stanisław at Skałka
ul. Skałeczna, 15

Stanisław was born to a gentry family in Szczepanów, a village in the Małopolska region, on July 26, 1030. Sent abroad for his education (to Paris or Liège, according to different sources), he returned to Poland and became one of the first native Polish bishops in the newly converted country, which embraced Latin Christianity in 966 with the baptism of the Piast prince Mieszko. Bishop Stanisław served first as an auxiliary bishop of Kraków and then as the city's Ordinary.

Stanisław was credited by pious tradition with one striking miracle during his years as the local bishop. As the story goes, Bishop Stanisław found himself in a dispute over a parcel of land along the Vistula River, near Lublin. The bishop claimed to have bought the property from its owner; on the owner's death, his heirs disputed the purchase and the king sided with the family. The bishop asked for three days to provide evidence for his claim, and spent those days in fasting and prayer. On the third day, dressed in his episcopal regalia, Bishop Stanisław went to the tomb of the deceased landowner and called him to life in order to bear witness to his sale of the property. After berating his three sons for their lie, the deceased man told the king that the property did indeed rightfully belong to the bishop of Kraków, and then returned to his repose in his tomb.

Shortly thereafter, Stanisław was accused of treason, and while the historical record is murky as to the source of the charge, it may have had to do with the king's harsh treatment of the unfaithful wives of noblemen who had been long absent at war. Citing the king's own infidelities, the bishop excommunicated the king, thus gravely weakening the monarch's position. King Bolesław responded by condemning the bishop to death for treason, and when his retainers would not touch Stanisław, Bolesław slew him while he was saying Mass at Skałka, dismembered his corpse, and threw the various body parts into a nearby pond. According to pious tradition, the body of Bishop Stanisław was then miraculously reassembled and given proper burial. Bolesław left for Hungary, never to return to Poland, and Stanisław became the country's patron saint, ultimately interred in a great silver casket at the center of Wawel Cathedral.

Skałka remains one of Poland's great shrines, and on May 8, the feast of St. Stanisław in the Polish liturgical calendar, the archbishop of Kraków annually leads a great procession of the saint's relics from Skałka to Wawel Cathedral.

A small Romanesque church at Skałka ("little rock" in Polish) dates back to the eleventh century and was named in honor of St. Michael. The Skałka church was rebuilt in Gothic style by King Kazimierz the Great in the fourteenth century, and was subsequently rebuilt in its current baroque style in the eighteenth century.

The high altar is decorated in a unique fashion, with six blue marble Corinthian columns. To the left of the high altar is the shrine of St. Stanisław, on what tradition claims as the site of his martyrdom. A glass case houses the block of wood upon which the bishop's body was dismembered, and above the altar is a *votum*, a thanksgiving offering, from Pope John Paul II: a golden pectoral cross.

To the right of the church, the pond where the martyr's remains were thrown is surrounded by a stone wall enclosing a staircase that pilgrims can descend to obtain "St. Stanisław water"; the pond includes a statue of the saint.

When Kraków was the royal capital of Poland, new kings would make a penitential pilgrimage to Skałka prior to their coronations. The Skałka church crypt is now used as the final resting place for Poles of distinction, reflecting a tradition that began with the fifteenth-century burial there of the historian and diplomat Jan Długosz. The most recent internment was of Nobel laureate Czesław Miłosz, who died in 2004.

The Altar of the Three Millennia

The Skałka complex is in the care of the Pauline fathers, whose seminary is just outside the entrance to the property. The site was enhanced in 2008 by the Altar of the Three Millennia, an amphitheater for public ceremonies honoring seven saints and heroes who shaped Poland's Catholic history from the late first millennium to the beginnings of the third. From left to right:

> *Father Augustyn Kordecki* (1603–1673), prior of the Jasna Góra monastery of the Black Madonna, who led the defense of Częstochowa during "the Deluge," the Swedish invasion of Poland in 1655.
>
> *St. Jadwiga* (1374–1399), the young queen whose marriage to the Lithuanian duke Władysław Jagiełło created the great Polish-Lithuanian commonwealth and whose benefactions helped create the Academy of Kraków, later the **Jagiellonian University;** canonized by John Paul II in Kraków in 1997.
>
> *St. Adalbert* [Wojciech] (956–997), a monk and bishop of Prague, later an evangelist in Hungary, Poland, and Prussia, where he was martyred by pagans; now buried in Gniezno, Poland's primatial see.
>
> *St. Stanisław* (1030–1079), martyred at Skałka and buried in **Wawel Cathedral.**

St. John Paul II (1920–2005).

St. Maria Faustina Kowalska (1905–1938), apostle of Divine Mercy, buried in the **Convent of the Sisters of Our Lady of Mercy** in **Łagiewniki.**

St. Jan Kanty (1390–1473), student and later professor at the Academy of Kraków, now patron saint of the Jagiellonian University, buried in the university parish church, the **Collegiate Church of St. Anne.** [C.G.]

St. Florian's

Pastoral Accompaniment, Środowisko,
and the Beginning of World Youth Day

In the late 1940s, Cardinal Adam Stefan Sapieha knew that the minds and hearts of Poland's young people were a crucial battleground in the Catholic Church's struggle with communism for the future of Poland. So the aristocratic

Jan Matejko Place—Grunwald Monument and St. Florian's

archbishop decided to create a second center of university chaplaincy in Kraków to complement the fine work being done by Father Jan Pietraszko at the **Collegiate Church of St. Anne,** near the **Jagiellonian University.** Located in the venerable parish of **St. Florian's,** a traditional home to Kraków's Catholic intellectuals, the new center would extend the reach of the archdiocesan campus ministry into the neighborhood of the academic institutions clustered around the *Plac Matejki* in the city's Kleparz district, just north of the Floriańska Gate and the Barbican: the **Academy of Fine Arts,** the **Kraków Polytechnic,** and the nearby student housing. Starting a new campus ministry at the height of Polish Stalinism, when the Party and the state it controlled were tightening the screws on the Church, would be no easy business. But Sapieha thought he had the man for the job in Father Karol Wojtyła, recently returned from doctoral studies in Rome.

In sending Father Wojtyła to St. Florian's in March 1949, Cardinal Sapieha hoped to meet an urgent immediate pastoral need in the archdiocese of Kraków. He certainly succeeded in doing that. What even so foresighted a man as Adam Stefan Sapieha could not have imagined was that, in sending Wojtyła to St. Florian's, he was planting the seeds of a revolution in the Catholic Church's ministry to young people, seeds that would eventually produce a new global event in the rhythm of Catholic life—World Youth Day.

THE DYNAMISM OF Pope John Paul II was not a special gift of the Holy Spirit, conferred on him when he accepted the Office of Peter on October 16, 1978. John Paul II was an exceptionally dynamic pope because he had been an exceptionally dynamic priest and bishop. The priest who became an innovative and successful diocesan bishop—a wonderful preparation for the papacy, as things turned out—was formed at St. Florian's, in a remarkable network of friendships that began here and that shaped Karol Wojtyła's thinking for the rest of his life.

Other popes of the nineteenth and twentieth centuries, asked to describe their critical early years in the priesthood, would have spoken of an academic or diplomatic career: teaching in a local or Roman seminary, working in the Roman Curia, or serving as a junior official in one of the Holy See's diplomatic missions abroad. John Paul II, asked the same question, offered a very different, and very telling, answer. He talked about his work with university students, and not only in the formal sense of being a catechist and confessor, but as a friend and companion on skiing, hiking, kayaking, and camping trips.

His native gifts, the harrowing experience of life under the Nazi occupation, and the work of grace in him had combined to create a striking maturity in Wojtyła by the time he was ordained a priest in 1946. That maturity was refined intellectually during his two years of graduate study in Rome, in 1946–48. Wojtyła's pastoral maturity and creativity were honed at St. Florian's, as he set about the mission Cardinal Sapieha had given him.

The times were not easy. Thanks to the ubiquitous communist "security forces," suspicion was a normal mode of self-protection: students often didn't know each other's surnames, open conversation was a danger, and every priest in Poland had a secret police agent watching his every move. In a world

St. John Paul II altar,
St. Florian's

without cell phones, text messaging, or instant communication, a world in which formal Catholic youth work was banned by the state under severe penalties, Karol Wojtyła began creating at St. Florian's networks of conversation, formation, and friendship that became zones of openness and freedom in the bleak, claustrophobic atmosphere of early 1950s Poland.

It was retail work at first, Father Wojtyła going to the dormitories, boardinghouses, convents, and other places where students lived, introducing himself, and inviting young men and women to St. Florian's for discussions about the existence of God and the spiritual character of the human person—two themes that amounted to a frontal assault on communist ideology. Later, this "young, poorly dressed, pious priest" (as one student at the time remembered him) asked some of his young charges to help form a parish choir at St. Florian's.

They began by singing Christmas carols at the very end of the Christmas season, and once the ice had been broken, Wojtyła taught them the basic elements of Gregorian chant, including the *Missa de Angelis,* which the new choir of young men and women began singing at the parish on Sundays.

Father Wojtyła ran what might be called a full-service campus ministry. He gave his young friends days of recollection to mark special events during the year, celebrated Mass for them on their name days (the Polish alternative to birthdays), and went to parties in their homes. He also celebrated special Masses for exam days and joined in the post-exam parties at night. All of this was in sharp contrast to the distance typically found between clergy and laity in Poland, especially in Stalinist Poland; for Wojtyła, however, this was what a priestly ministry to the young meant—accompanying young people in their lives as a friend, a counselor, and a moral leader who could challenge his followers and friends to make good decisions about their lives and futures.

Wojtyła's students at first called themselves *Rodzinka,* or "Little Family," and what began as a group of fewer than twenty men and women quickly expanded by invitation (Wojtyła suggesting that this or that person he'd met be invited into the group) and along family lines. After a memorable trip to see the crocus fields near Zakopane during Easter Week 1952, Wojtyła's young people began to call him *Wujek,* "Uncle," a kind of Stalinist-era nom de guerre that protected both priest and students from secret police ferrets and snoopers.

It was the name the friends he made at St. Florian's would call him until his death in 2005.

FATHER WOJTYŁA LEFT St. Florian's in 1951, moving to the Dean's House at Kanonicza 21, near Wawel, to work on the habilitation thesis that would qualify him as a university professor; many of his young friends followed him to St. Catherine's Church near Skałka and Kazimierz, when he began to celebrate his daily Mass there. Yet even after Wojtyła moved out of St. Florian's, what began there as *Rodzinka* continued to expand until it formed a network of some two hundred friends who, at Wojtyła's suggestion, began in the 1960s to call themselves *Środowisko;* the word is difficult to translate from the Polish, but it conveys the sense of "environment" or "milieu." For more than forty years, Karol Wojtyła, as priest, bishop, and pope, remained faithful to what he always called "my *Środowisko*." These were the men and women with whom he hiked and camped, skied and kayaked throughout his years in Kraków—men and women whose marriages he had solemnized and whose children he had baptized. Perhaps his closest friend in *Środowisko* was Jerzy Ciesielski, a great skiing and kayaking instructor, who died in a boating accident outside Khartoum in 1970 while teaching engineering in an exchange program at a local university. When Ciesielski's wife, Danuta, and her daughter Maria brought Jurek Ciesielski's ashes home for burial, a journey that took them through Rome, Cardinal Wojtyła, in the Eternal City for a meeting, met them at the airport with a car and driver, celebrated Mass for them, and asked that the funeral in Kraków be delayed so that he could celebrate the Requiem Mass.

In his *Środowisko,* Karol Wojtyła refined the pastoral

strategy he would call "accompaniment." Because he had gotten to know his friends' lives "from the inside," as one of the earliest members of *Rodzinka* once put it, he was in a privileged position to walk with his friends along the pathways of their lives, in open and frank conversations that deepened friendships rather than straining them. He was a moral reference point for his friends and did not hesitate to be a challenging counselor and confessor. But the pastoral stress (which complemented one of the main themes in Wojtyła's work in philosophical ethics) was always on personal responsibility. He was not the decider for his friends; they must be their own deciders, he insisted, if they were to be true to the moral dignity built into them as human persons and as Christians.

The friendships that began to form at St. Florian's in the late 1940s and early 1950s stayed green for decades. In August 2000, amidst all the other activity of the great Jubilee of 2000, three generations of *Środowisko* (including the grandchildren of the original members of *Rodzinka*) came for a Jubilee visit to Castel Gandolfo, the papal summer residence in the Alban Hills outside Rome. (They brought a kayak into the papal villa's courtyard, and the reunion was immediately dubbed "Dry Kayaks at Castel Gandolfo.") Their meeting was originally scheduled for a half-hour, but John Paul insisted on meeting everyone present, more than a hundred people—and then repeating the personal greetings by saying good night to everyone personally, after which the eighty-year-old pontiff finally walked haltingly into the villa, the small grandchildren of his hiking and kayaking friends trailing him in a ragged line, "like the Good Shepherd and the sheep," as one veteran of the choir loft at St. Florian's put it later.

Three years later, when Krzysztof Rybicki, a longtime *Śro-dowisko* member, was dying from cancer, John Paul II called him in his hospital room. "Krysiu," he asked the dying man, "do you remember how we used to sing carols together? We can sing together even now." And they did. Two years after that, Krzysztof Rybicki's widow, Maria, and seventy other *Środowisko* members did the same for *Wujek*. They came to Rome for his funeral in outdoor gear, planning to sleep in parks, unsure whether they could get tickets to the funeral Mass. In the event, thanks to John Paul II's longtime secretary, then-Archbishop Stanisław Dziwisz, they were seated, in their hiking clothes, just behind the heads of state and government in front of St. Peter's Basilica, to say goodbye to the man they had first met at St. Florian's: the man who had taken the lessons he had learned with them (and, he would insist, from them) to the entire world.

ONE OF THE many striking things about the pontificate of John Paul II was that so much of it was previewed in Kraków, during Wojtyła's years as priest and bishop. His pastoral pilgrimages around the world (to take just one example) were global extensions of the extensive parish visitations that were a major part of his pastoral program as archbishop of Kraków. Asked once about these Cracovian "previews" of his pontificate, John Paul replied that it all seemed rather obvious to him: if the Holy Spirit had seen fit to call the archbishop of Kraków to be the Bishop of Rome, that must mean that there was something in the experience of the Church of Kraków that was important for the world Church.

The most dramatic of these "transfers" from Kraków to Rome, and from there to the world, was World Youth Day—the global youth festival that John Paul II inaugurated in 1984 and which has become a significant expression of the universality of the Church as well as a regular marker in the global rhythms of Catholic life.

It is probably a fair guess that most of the world's bishops didn't think much of John Paul's World Youth Day initiative when he first announced it. Young people, they had concluded, simply weren't interested in high-octane Catholicism. They lived in a different conceptual and moral universe and spoke a different language; youth culture seemed far removed from Catholicism. In the late twentieth century, young ministry was something of a lost cause. John Paul II disagreed. The Pope who, three months before his death, would sit a *Środowisko* grandchild next to him at dinner and say, "Tell me what the kids are interested in today," didn't believe youth ministry was a hopeless proposition. He believed that, for all the changes in culture, human beings hadn't changed since his days at St. Florian's, and that young people still wanted to be summoned to lead heroic lives.

And that, it seems, was the insight that created World Youth Day. Unlike those who thought that "Catholic Lite"—Catholicism dumbed down doctrinally and morally—was the only possible strategy for youth ministry, the Pope who as a young priest had gotten to know his young friends' lives "from inside," through the pastoral method he called "accompaniment," thought that what young people wanted was challenge and adventure: the challenge and adventure of being more than contemporary youth culture thought they could be; the challenge and adventure of being more than bundles of desires; the challenge and adventure of learning what was right—what made for true happiness—and then conforming their lives to that.

In a world that constantly pandered to the young—in modes of dress, language, and advertising; in lowering academic and behavioral expectations—John Paul did not pander. He challenged, and his challenge rang true because of his transparent honesty: he did not ask anything of the young that he had not asked of himself. And at the end, as in his homily at the closing Mass of World Youth Day in Toronto in 2002, he asked nothing less of young people than to stake their lives on the cause in which he was, manifestly, pouring out his own life:

> Although I have lived through much darkness, under harsh totalitarian regimes, I have seen enough evidence to be unshakably convinced that no difficulty, no fear is so great that it can completely suffocate the hope that springs eternal in the hearts of the young. You are our hope; the young are our hope. Do not let that hope die! Stake your lives on it! We are not the sum of our weaknesses and failures; we are the sum of the Father's love for us and our real capacity to become the image of his Son.

Holiness, he insisted, "is not a question of age." Holiness is "a matter of living in the Holy Spirit." And that grace was available to everyone, of any age. It was the summation of what he had taught, and the challenge he had offered, for more than fifty years: Never, ever settle for anything less than the spiritual and moral grandeur that the grace of God makes possible in your life. You will fail, and you will fall. But that is no reason to lower the bar of expectation. Get up, dust yourself off, and seek forgiveness through the sacrament of Reconciliation. But don't ever settle for anything less than the greatness that Christ makes possible in you, through the Holy Spirit.

It was a message and a challenge that first took shape at St. Florian's. And in that sense, World Youth Day did not begin in Rome in 1984. It began at St. Florian's in 1949, among the young people who would later be known as Karol Wojtyła's *Środowisko*.

St. Florian's

Kleparz, now a Cracovian neighborhood known for its open-air farmers' market, was originally a town in its own right. Founded in 1184, Kleparz is located just north of the Barbican, the northernmost point of the fortifications that once surrounded the Old Town and one of the sole surviving remnants of what was once a great complex of high walls and defense towers, surrounded by a moat. The Barbican, which has 130 openings for marksmen defending Kraków against marauders or invaders, is itself a stone's throw from the last of the city's great medieval tower gates, the Floriańska Gate, named, like the street it heads, for St. Florian, the city's patron saint prior to St. Stanisław.

To the north of both the Floriańska Gate and the Barbican is the *Plac Matejki* [Matejko Place], named in honor of the Pol-

Basilica of the Assumption of Our Lady (*Mariacki*)

St. Maximilian Kolbe altar, Basilica of St. Francis

Icon of Our Lady of
Perpetual Help, Basilica
of the Presentation of the
Blessed Virgin Mary

Sanctuary, Wawel Cathedral

Courtyard, Royal Castle

Main Altar, Basilica of St. Michael and St. Stanisław

St. Catherine's Church

Creation window (Wyspiański), Basilica of St. Francis

Wit Stwosz altarpiece,
Basilica of the Assumption
of Our Lady (*Mariacki*)

Organ, Ark Church

Chapel of Our Lady of Fatima, Ark Church

Miraculous Madonna, Kalwaria Zebrzydowska

Eleventh Station chapel,
Kalwaria Zebrzydowska

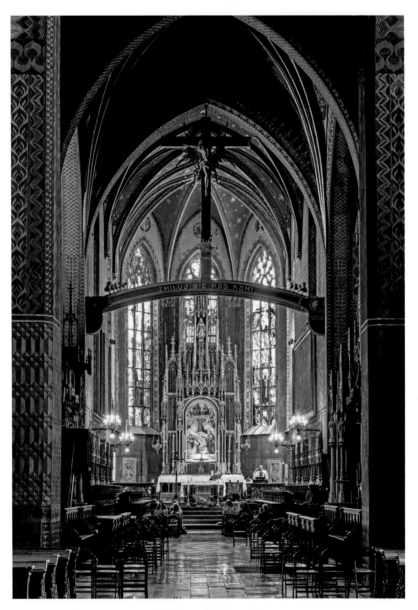

Basilica of St. Francis

St. Florian's

ish historical painter whose nineteenth-century work played an important role in keeping the idea of "Poland" alive when the Polish state no longer existed. The proverbial starving artist become distinguished and honored cultural icon Jan Matejko (1838–1893) was the rector of Kraków's Academy of Fine Arts. In addition to creating his own works, Matejko, a pious and patriotic Pole, was a benefactor of and contributor to major nineteenth-century decorative projects in Kraków, including the interior of the *Mariacki* basilica in the *Rynek Główny* and the **Collegium Novum** of the **Jagiellonian University.**

At the center of *Plac Matejki* is the Grunwald Monument, which commemorates the victory of King Władysław Jagiełło (portrayed in a great equestrian statue) over the Teutonic Knights at the 1410 Battle of Grunwald, which checked the power of the aggressive monastic brotherhood in the Baltic

Floriańska Gate

regions and helped secure Polish sovereignty. Built in 1910 with funds provided by Ignacy Paderewski, the patriotic Polish pianist, composer, and statesman who would briefly become prime minister of the Second Polish Republic in 1919, the Grunwald Monument was wrecked during the occupation by Nazis offended at the idea of Slavs defeating Teutons and rebuilt after the war.

St. Florian's Church
ul. Warszawska, 1

The original church on this site was built shortly after Poland's conversion to Christianity, around A.D. 1000. The church dedication derives from Kraków's aspirations to become a religious as well as political and commercial center—a goal whose realization required a patron saint. So in 1184, the city authorities requested and received the relics of St. Florian (who had been born in today's Austria), which were then entrusted to the church in Kleparz that now bears his name. St. Florian's status as city patron was short-lived, given the ascendancy of the cult of St. Stanisław, but St. Florian's remained one of Kraków's most important parishes for centuries: the great processions accompanying the coronations and burials of Polish kings began at St. Florian's and ended at Wawel Cathedral.

Born in A.D. 250, St. Florian was a Roman legionary, a member of a unit whose chief mission was firefighting. After defying imperial orders to worship the ancient gods of Rome, Florian was condemned to death by being burned at the stake. According to tradition, he said, while standing on the pyre, "I will climb to heaven on the flames." His executioners decided to alter the sentence and drowned him with a millstone around his neck. He remains today the patron of firefighters and chimney sweeps, and in iconography is usually portrayed in front of a burning building. According to local legend, the site of the church was chosen when the carriage carrying his relics mysteriously stopped here, the horses refusing to go any farther—a supernatural sign, the townspeople decided, that the church in honor of their new patron saint should be built here.

The church burned down repeatedly over the centuries and was severely damaged during the seventeenth-century Swedish siege of Kraków, "the Deluge." Yet St. Florian's remained intact during the great citywide conflagration of 1528—a sign to Cracovians that the church's patron was protecting his parish.

Today's baroque church, built of stone and brick, was a benefaction of the noble Potocki family and dates to the late seventeenth century, after the Swedish siege was lifted. Damaged during World War II, it was rebuilt immediately after the war.

The twin copper towers are an eighteenth-century addition; centered below them is a stout, domed neo-baroque porch capped with an early twentieth-century cupola. The vaulting in the three-aisled interior is especially prominent in the sanctuary or presbytery. The centerpiece of the expansive, gilded baroque altar is a painting of St. Florian; a baroque crucifix is suspended from the ceiling between the nave and the sanctuary. The neo-rococo stucco and murals were added in the twentieth century.

John Paul II elevated the church to the rank of a minor basilica in 1999 and visited the church during his last papal pilgrimage to Poland, September 18, 2002. He is remembered in St. Florian's at a shrine to the left of the sanctuary and in a memorial on the facade of the rectory (located to the left of the church), where he lived from March 1949 until September 1951.

Jan Matejko Academy of Fine Arts in Kraków
Plac Matejki, 13

Poland's oldest school of fine arts, the Academy of Fine Arts, was founded in 1818 as part of the Jagiellonian University but became an independent institution in 1926; it was renamed in honor of its most famous student and rector, Jan Matejko (himself the teacher of such great Polish artists as Stanisław Wyspiański and Józef Mehoffer), in 1979. Closed by the German occupation during World War II, the Academy reconstituted itself underground during the war years. Although the Academy

Barbican and Kraków Institute of Fine Arts

strove to resume normal operations at the war's end, many of its prewar faculty members had been executed by the Nazis or had died in concentration camps. One of the Academy's rectors in the postcommunist period, Stanisław Rodziński, a distinguished painter, was a member of John Paul II's *Środowisko*.

The Tadeusz Kościuszko University of Technology in Kraków
ul. Warszawska, 24

Known to all as the Kraków Polytechnic, the university traces some of its component schools and programs back to 1834, although the institution in its present form was established in 1946. Granted full autonomy in 1954, the university was named in honor of the Polish and American hero Tadeusz Kościuszko, a

Kraków Polytechnic

skilled engineer, in 1976. Today the university is composed of several faculties, including architecture, chemical engineering and technology, civil engineering, electrical and computer engineering, environmental engineering, mechanical engineering, physics, mathematics, and computer science. Piotr Malecki, a distinguished physicist and the self-described *"enfant terrible of Środowisko,"* was a longtime faculty member of the Polytechnic, whose graduates included Stanisław Rybicki, an original member of *Rodzinka*, the group of young adults at St. Florian's that grew into Karol Wojtyła's *Środowisko*.

The Rhapsodic Theater
ul. Warszawska, 5

The Rhapsodic Theater was founded in August 1941 by Mieczysław Kotlarczyk and Karol Wojtyła in the "catacombs"

Rhapsodic Theater memorial, Warszawska 5

apartment at Tyniecka 10 in Dębniki; in addition to Kotlarczyk, who was very much the leader of the enterprise and the definer of its unique aesthetic, the original troupe included Wojtyła, Krystyna Dębowska, Halina Królikiewicz (another refugee from Wadowice), and Danuta Michałowska. Performing clandestinely around Kraków, the Rhapsodists understood their art as part of the cultural resistance to the occupation, helping strengthen Polish spirits through the disciplined performance of some of the country's greatest poetry and drama, which they undertook (and their audiences watched) at risk of their lives.

Absent Karol Wojtyła, who served as its unofficial chaplain, the Rhapsodic Theater continued after the war until it was suppressed by the communist authorities in 1953; its home from 1947 to 1951 was here, at Warszawska 5. Reopened during the 1956 political thaw in Poland, it was finally closed by the communists in 1967, over the protests of Cardinal Karol Wojtyła, who had learned something about fighting tyranny with the weapons of culture from his Rhapsodist friends and colleagues. [C.G.]

The Metropolitan Curia
and the Planty

*The Good Shepherd
in the Modern World*

During the sixteen years that Karol Wojtyła led the Archdiocese of Kraków as vicar capitular (apostolic administrator) and metropolitan archbishop, he often conducted the more sensitive aspects of archdiocesan business in walks with his colleagues and associates along the **Planty,** the great greensward that defines the perimeter of Kraków's Old Town. Doing so was not so much a matter of the physical exercise Wojtyła enjoyed as it was of security. It was a lot harder for the secret police to monitor his conversations when he was outdoors.

As archbishop of Kraków, Karol Wojtyła was constantly harassed by the Polish authorities. The secret police (the *Służba Bezpieczeństwa,* called "the SB") made every effort to impede his work, in a vast expenditure of money and personnel that, objectively, constituted a great act of theft: the ongoing robbery of civil society by the state. The rooms at **Franciszkańska 3,** the **Metropolitan Curia,** where Wojtyła had both his residence and his office, were electronically bugged. The

Chapel, Archbishop's Residence

SB constantly tried to recruit his co-workers and staff as in-formers. The archbishop himself was watched twenty-four hours a day, 365 days a year, by SB agents, whose reports added to the thickening Wojtyła file at the headquarters of the so-called security services—files that included reports not only on his public activity but on such personal minutiae as his shaving habits and the urgent question of who bought his underwear and shined his shoes. Department IV of the SB, devoted to counter-Church activities, was formed within the SB in June 1962; eleven years later, in November 1973, In-dependent Group D was formed within Department IV and given the mandate to "disintegrate" the Catholic Church in Poland. One of Independent Group D's principal targets was Cardinal Karol Wojtyła, described in one SB report as a "very dangerous ideological opponent."

As Wojtyła's longtime secretary, Stanisław Dziwisz, once observed, the relationship between the Catholic Church and the communist party in Poland was nothing like the relationship between the governing party and the opposition in a democracy. This was something dramatically, radically different. It was "we" and "they," "us" and "them." It was all war, all the time—a non-adjudicable struggle that would only be resolved when one side won and the other lost.

Despite these extraordinary circumstances—and, perhaps, in some way because of them—Karol Wojtyła conducted one of the great episcopal ministries of the twentieth century in Kraków. Inspired by the example of the "unbroken prince," Cardinal Sapieha, himself a modern embodiment of the Stanisław tradition of the bishop of Kraków as *defensor civitatis,* the people's last line of defense in the protection of their rights, Wojtyła fit Kraków perfectly, his sensibilities and skills extraordinarily well attuned to his diocese and the challenges facing his people.

THE FIRST FOUR years of Karol Wojtyła's leadership of the venerable see of St. Stanisław coincided with the Second Vatican Council (1962–65), the most important event in Catholic history since the sixteenth century. First, as one of the youngest bishops at Vatican II, and later as one of the Council's intellectual leaders, Karol Wojtyła had a significant impact on the deliberations of some twenty-five hundred bishops, many of whom came to know his special qualities during the Vatican II years. Wojtyła received as well as gave during the four years of the Council, later noting that Vatican II had been a kind of second graduate school in theology for him. In Rome during the Council's autumn working periods, and at meetings between the formal sessions of Vatican II, Wojtyła befriended some of the great theologians of the mid-twentieth century Catholic renaissance, forming a special bond with the French Jesuit Henri de Lubac. Vatican II was also a decisive experience of the universality of the Catholic Church for Wojtyła; it was at the Council, for example, that his fascination with Africa and African Catholic leaders began, as he got a personal taste of the New Testament freshness of African Catholicism.

At Vatican II, Wojtyła worked hardest on what became *Gaudium et Spes* (Joy and Hope), the Council's Pastoral Constitution on the Church in the Modern World. There, his imprint is unmistakable in two paragraphs that became, in time, the most frequently cited conciliar texts in the teaching of Pope John Paul II. *Gaudium et Spes* 22 is a concise (and precise) statement of Wojtyła's Christian humanism, his Christian understanding of the human person: "It is only in the mystery of the Word made flesh that the mystery of man truly becomes clear. . . . Christ the Lord, Christ the New Adam, in the very revelation of the mystery of the Father and of his love, fully reveals man to himself and brings to light his most high calling." *Gaudium et Spes* 24 then applies that incarnational humanism to the moral life, in a concise statement of the "Law of the Gift" built into the human condition, a central theme in Wojtyła's philosophical ethics: "Man can fully discover his true self only in a sincere giving of himself." Self-giving, not self-assertion, is the royal road to human flourishing and happiness—or, in biblical terms, beatitude. Wojtyła thought that could be demonstrated by a careful and disciplined reflection on moral action, the dynamics of human moral choosing. The confirmation of that Law of the Gift, however, came from divine revelation, for it was Jesus Christ, the Son who obediently made himself into a sacrificial gift to his Father, who displayed the full truth of our humanity at its noblest.

Christian humanism, then, was the ground on which Karol Wojtyła, as archbishop of Kraków, proposed to fight the battle for the soul of Poland and for his people's future. He would challenge the false, atheistic humanism of the communist project with a truer, deeper, more compelling humanism: the view of the human person disclosed by Christ the Lord, in his Transfiguration and Resurrection.

WOJTYŁA'S PROGRAM AS archbishop was an extension of this Christian humanism and of the humanistic dimension of his multilayered soul. He summoned an archdiocesan synod— including lay people as well as clergy—to read the documents of Vatican II, to ponder their meaning for the pastoral life of the Church in Kraków, and to make decisions about archdiocesan structures and programs: a nine-year process that he would solemnly close in June 1979 as Bishop of Rome. The archbishop himself wrote a *vademecum* of key Vatican II texts to help guide the synod's deliberations; his running commentary on selections from the sixteen documents of the Council was later published in book form as *Sources of Renewal*.

As the synod unfolded, so did Wojtyła's ministry as archbishop, which he built around seven priorities.

The first was religious freedom, symbolized in the struggle for a church in Nowa Huta, the steel-milling town built

outside Kraków after World War II and the first such set-
tlement in Polish history deliberately constructed without a
church. Poland's communist authorities were determined to
reduce Catholicism to a private matter of lifestyle choice; in
the battle for the church at Nowa Huta, and at great public
religious events like the annual Corpus Christi procession,
Karol Wojtyła met that challenge by demonstrating the inherently public character of Christian faith and the absurdity
of a Polish public square stripped of religious conviction.

Wojtyła's second priority was to strengthen seminary education and provide for the continuing education of young
priests—his junior officers in the contest between Church
and Party for the Polish future. In addition to reforming the
intellectual preparation of Kraków's future priests, Wojtyła
took their personal and spiritual formation personally, meeting frequently with his seminarians and then holding regular gatherings of each ordination class (sometimes on the ski
slopes) during their early years in the priesthood.

Youth ministry was, not surprisingly, Wojtyła's third priority. The former university chaplain went out of his way to
support pastoral initiatives that gave young men and women
opportunities for Christian living and Christian formation,
including the Oasis summer camps and the "Light and Life"
movement, two Catholic responses to the communist regime's ban on Catholic youth organizations. Adopting another method from his years at St. Florian's, the archbishop
also encouraged altar boy and parish choir gatherings that
included religious instruction as well as recreation.

Karol Wojtyła's lifelong concern for family ministry
came to its fullest institutional expression during his years

as archbishop of Kraków. The young priest-philosopher who had made marriage preparation a key part of his ministry to his *Środowisko* and to others now created Poland's first diocesan institute on marriage and the family (housing it in the archiepiscopal office/residence complex at Franciszkańska 3) and made training for marriage preparation an essential part of the formation of seminarians and the ongoing education of priests. In addition, Wojtyła created an archdiocesan fund to support unwed mothers who wished to bear their children rather than submit to abortion (the typical method of "birth control" in communist countries), urging local convents to care for these women until they had borne their children and were prepared to raise them as single mothers. In all of this, Wojtyła was laying the groundwork for the Theology of the Body he would explicate as pope—an approach to human love and marriage that would revolutionize campus ministry and marriage preparation in the more alert parts of the world Church.

A man of constant conversation, Karol Wojtyła made ongoing dialogue with the academics and intellectuals of Kraków the fifth priority of his ministry as archbishop. He had close friends among the Kraków Catholic intelligentsia, and when a distinguished scholar such as Jacek Woźniakowski (who would eventually become the first noncommunist mayor of Kraków after the Revolution of 1989) could not get the position that his accomplishments would normally have gained him at the Jagiellonian University, he was hired by the independent Catholic newspaper to which Wojtyła contributed and which he protected, *Tygodnik Powszechny* (Universal Weekly). Wojtyła's work with intellectuals was not limited to

Catholics, though. He deliberately brought nonbelievers into the circle of his conversation, thus helping lay some of the foundations for the broad-based Solidarity movement of the future.

Wojtyła also insisted on giving priority to the ministry of charity. Normal Catholic charitable institutions—hospitals, nursing homes, residences for unwed mothers and orphans, medical clinics, institutions for the handicapped and the mentally ill—were forbidden in communist Poland. Wojtyła made that ban into an opportunity to enrich parish life in the archdiocese of Kraków by establishing "pastoral charity teams" in each parish, whose members would identify and care for the local sick and the needy—and would do so without regard to religious affiliation or the lack thereof. Those working in the ministry of charity through Kraków's parishes were given regular catechetical instruction, thus linking this essential social work to ongoing Christian formation. Wojtyła also made special efforts to bring the elderly and the ill—typically marginalized in communist societies—into the mainstream of local Catholic life.

All of this came to a focal point in the seventh priority of Wojtyła's stewardship on the archdiocese of Kraków: his extensive program of parish visitations, during which he would often move into a local community for days, sharing its life, blessing new graves, offering a special Mass and blessing for married couples, celebrating the sacrament of Confirmation, meeting with the local sisters and lay volunteers, and devoting special attention to the parish religion teachers. Karol Wojtyła's parish visits were far more a local retreat than a formality mandated by church law; from his point of view they were

Drawing room, Archbishop's Residence

opportunities to both explain and live out the Christian humanism that was his counter to Polish state propaganda and
the communist culture of the lie that surrounded his people
like a thick, choking fog.

THE CENTER OF all this activity was the Metropolitan Curia
in the Kraków Old Town. Often called by its address, "Franciszkańska Three," it was a familiar venue to Karol Wojtyła,
who had been hidden there as an underground seminarian
in 1944–45. Things had changed, of course, since Archbishop
Sapieha had turned his drawing rooms into dormitories and
classrooms for his clandestine seminarians. But at Franciszkańska 3, Karol Wojtyła lived simply, if not quite in the spar-
tan ruggedness of the war years.

He had a small suite of three rooms, in which the only

picture was a photograph of his parents. He rose early, prayed for an hour, and did his intellectual work—the preparation of sermons and pastoral letters; writing his essays, books, poems, and plays—at a work table in the residence chapel, before the reposed Blessed Sacrament. He reserved a daily two-hour period, between 11:00 a.m. and 1:00 p.m., for visitors; anyone who wanted to see the cardinal archbishop of Kraków would simply come, take a seat in a parlor, and be seen in turn. The sisters who cooked for the household were renowned for their *bigos,* a classic Polish stew; Christmas caroling parties with his *Środowisko* at his residence (during which he displayed his remarkable knowledge of traditional Polish songs down to the last verse) were, among other things, opportunities to indulge the cardinal's sweet tooth.

He had neither money nor bank account of his own and wore his clothes until they were threadbare. Dedicated to his work, he also worked in a disciplined way, and, with his *Środowisko* friends, took the skiing and kayaking vacations that were essential for recharging his spiritual and emotional energies.

Every Friday, and every day during Lent, he crossed ul. Franciszkańska to pray the Stations of the Cross in the **Basilica of St. Francis of Assisi,** in a chapel that featured striking modern renderings of the traditional *Via Crucis* by Józef Mehoffer.

As he became one of the leading figures in world Catholicism during the 1970s, he traveled extensively, to Rome and to the Polish diaspora in North America and Australia. Yet while he enjoyed travel as an opportunity to meet new people and engage in new conversations, he also welcomed the return

Chapel of the Stations of the Cross, Basilica of St. Francis

to his "beloved Kraków." It was where, by his own choice, he would have spent out his life.

Divine Providence, however, had other plans.

IT WAS DURING his Cracovian contest with communism that Karol Wojtyła honed the arguments about Christian human-ism and the free society he would later deploy on a world stage. As a young priest-philosopher he had taught Catholic social ethics in the Silesian seminary in Kraków, so he was well versed in the Catholic social doctrine tradition of Pope Leo XIII and Pope Pius XI (a former nuncio to Poland much admired by Poles for his refusal to leave Warsaw in 1920 when the Red Army was closing in). And from that tradition, as refined by his own reflections, Wojtyła learned, and taught, that Catholic social doctrine is not for Catholics only. Based as it is on the claim that there are truths built into the world and into human beings, truths than can be discerned by reason, Catholic social teaching as Wojtyła understood it (and as Leo XIII and Pius XI understood it) had a *public* character: it made arguments about freedom and justice in a grammar and vocabulary that could be engaged by anyone willing to make the effort.

Thus Wojtyła's contest with communism during his years as archbishop of Kraków—like the editorial stance taken by *Tygodnik Powszechny* and the articles that the only real newspaper in Poland published—was not in any sense sectarian. The Gospel shed important light on the dignity of the human person, to be sure. Yet that light illuminated some basic truths about social, political, and economic life that all people of goodwill could grasp.

Here was ecumenism in the fullest sense of the term: the Church, secure in its convictions about its own God-given rights, openly and vigorously defending the freedom of all.

The Metropolitan Curia and the Planty

The Planty

The circumference of Kraków's Old Town is defined by the Planty, a ring of walking paths some two and a half miles in length, built on the land that had once supported the walls and towers of the medieval fortifications that stood between the

Metropolitan Curia and Pontifical John Paul II University

city and invaders. The full park surrounding the Planty's pathways includes fifty-two acres of landscaped fields and gardens embellished with monuments and fountains.

After the Third Polish Partition of 1795, when Kraków was under Austrian rule, the ancient and by then crumbling Old City walls were razed as part of a lengthy urban renewal program conducted between 1822 and 1847—and as a reminder to the local population not to attempt any rebellion against the Austrian authorities. Thanks to the intervention of a Jagiellonian University professor, Feliks Radwański, parts of the old walls can still be seen today; it was Radwański who convinced the Austrians to preserve the Floriańska Gate, its immediately adjacent walls, and the nearby Barbican—the most impressive fortress rondel in central Europe.

The Metropolitan Curia and Archbishop's Residence
ul. Franciszkańska, 3

In 1596, Giovanni Paolo Mucante, master of ceremonies to the papal legate Cardinal Henrico Gaetano, wrote: "If there were no Rome, Kraków would be Rome"—a tribute to the denseness of the city's Catholicism, with its many churches, its abundance of the tombs of the canonized or beatified, and its rich array of religious communities: Dominicans, Norbertines, Franciscans, Jesuits, Paulines, Benedictines, Camaldolese, Carmelites, Felicians, and Cistercians, to name but a few.

The Metropolitan Curia at Franciszkańska 3, the office and

Drawing room, Archbishop's Residence

residence of the archbishops of Kraków, holds an honored place in this very Catholic environment. Here young Karol Wojtyła had lived for over half a year as an underground seminarian, hidden from the Gestapo. Here he was ordained a priest in the residence chapel, on November 1, 1946. Here he lived and worked during most of his tenure as archbishop of Kraków. It was to this place that he returned, to stay in his old rooms (kept as he had left them in 1978) during his pilgrimages to the city as pope; and here is the iconic window, just above the entrance, from which John Paul II spoke to the young during his epic June 1979 papal pilgrimage. Here the people of Kraków came immediately after his death on April 2, 2005, leaving a mountain of flowers and candles that reached above the window from which he had once greeted them.

Prior to the thirteenth century, when the episcopal residence was moved here, the bishops of Kraków lived in a house in Wawel, near the cathedral. Like many other buildings in the Old Town, the bishop's residence was repeatedly damaged by fires; in the fifteenth century, a conflagration destroyed everything but the building's stone cellars and Gothic portals. Rebuilt by architect Gabriel Słoński around 1567, the complex was completed by two wings and a courtyard with an arcaded loggia in Renaissance style. In 1642–47, renovations by Bishop Piotr Gembicki added rusticated portals and a staircase to the palace, bringing the site's general appearance close to what it is today.

The complex was rebuilt and improved after the Swedish "Deluge" of 1655. In 1817–20, Bishop Jan Paweł Woronicz had the palace renovated by architect Szczepan Humbert. In response to the Third Polish Partition, the bishop used sixteen rooms of the Metropolitan Curia to exhibit national mementos and historic paintings. In 1850, another citywide fire burned most of the bishop's exhibit, including furnishings and his historic collections. Architect Tomasz Pryliński supervised the subsequent rebuilding and renovation, completed in 1884.

Today's complex at Franciszkańska 3 is a well-preserved example of nineteenth-century architecture, with a few remaining Renaissance and baroque elements. The arcaded courtyard now features a statue of Pope John Paul II, presented in May 1980 by artist Jole Sensi Croci.

Sapieha Memorial, Basilica of St. Francis of Assisi

The Basilica of St. Francis of Assisi
ul. Franciszkańska, 2

Directly across the street from Franciszkańska 3 is the Franciscan basilica, named in honor of the *Poverello* of Assisi, which dates back to the thirteenth century. Its precise origins have been lost to history, but a church on this site was consecrated before 1269 and witnessed many notable events, including the baptism and coronation in 1386 of Queen Jadwiga's husband, King Władysław Jagiełło. Little remains from that period beyond a ribbed thirteenth-century vault.

Renovated in the fifteenth century, the church was re-created in a new and unique configuration: a Greek Cross with an asymmetrical nave. Amidst other citywide fires and calamities, the great fire of 1850 did the most damage to the church, destroying both the church's fabric and many precious records and artifacts. The church was then reconstructed as the first brick-and-sandstone building in the city and reconsecrated on June 14, 1908, by the auxiliary bishop of Kraków, Anatol Nowak. On February 23, 1920, the church was elevated to the rank of a minor basilica.

Today's interior is neo-Gothic with some remaining Gothic elements. Polychrome decorates the presbytery and transept. The principal stained glass windows, featuring floral motifs that form a hymn to St. Francis, were created by the polymath artistic genius Stanisław Wyspiański and installed after the 1850 fire; the great window over the facade is Wyspiański's striking rendering of God the Father in the act of creation.

Today's nave includes, on the right, a memorial to the Franciscan "martyr of charity," Maximilian Kolbe, who lived in the adjacent Franciscan monastery from 1919 to 1922.

The chapel to the left of the nave includes the famous Mehoffer *Via Crucis,* before which Cardinal Wojtyła frequently prayed the Stations of the Cross during his years as archbishop of Kraków, and the relics of Blessed Aniela Salawa, a domestic servant who died in 1922 and was beatified by John Paul II on August 13, 1991.

To the left of the main entrance is a starkly modern statue of Cardinal Adam Stefan Sapieha, described as "the archbishop of the long, dark night of occupation," commissioned by Cardinal Karol Wojtyła and erected despite the resistance of the communist authorities.

Tygodnik Powszechny Offices
ul. Wiślna, 12

Cardinal Adam Stefan Sapieha established the newspaper *Tygodnik Powszechny* (Universal Weekly) as World War II was

Turowicz Memorial, offices of Tygodnik Powszechny

drawing to an end, and its first issue was published on March 24, 1945. The paper's founding editor in chief, Jerzy Turowicz, served until his death in 1999.

Housed in a building adjacent to the Metropolitan Curia and near the Jagiellonian University along the Planty, *Tygodnik Powszechny* was one of the most notable, and redoubtable, "free voices" behind the Iron Curtain. Closed in 1953 after Turowicz refused to run a government-mandated obituary of Joseph Stalin, the newspaper recovered its independence in the 1956 Polish political "thaw" and remained a tenacious defender of freedom until the collapse of communism in the Revolution of 1989.

Karol Wojtyła was a regular contributor during his years as priest and bishop in Kraków, and had the paper sent to him in Rome when he became pope. As Poland's most respected, uncensored journalistic outlet during the communist period, *Tygodnik Powszechny* attracted a distinguished roster of authors to its pages; after Czesław Miłosz received the 1980 Nobel Prize for Literature while living in exile in the United States, his poems, which had long appeared in the paper, were published exclusively in *Tygodnik Powszechny*. The paper's offices were a center of free discussion during the communist period. Many of those who had written for the paper played important roles in the formation of Solidarity in 1980–81, and during the turmoil of the 1980s the paper was a reliable and uncensored vehicle for the teachings of Pope John Paul II.

A bronze memorial on the exterior of Wiślna 12 honors the work of Jerzy Turowicz, as does a street named in his memory in the Łagiewniki-Borek Fałęcki district. [C.G.]

The Main Square and the Royal Mile

The Spaciousness of the Church

The contest for Poland's soul between the Polish people and the Catholic Church, on the one hand, and the Polish state controlled by the Polish Communist Party, on the other, was fought on many fronts. It was fought in the home and the classroom, in factories and offices, in sparsely populated rural regions and dense urban areas; above all, it was fought in minds and hearts. Kraków's **Main Market Square,** the *Rynek Główny,* and the **Royal Mile** that runs through the Square, from ul. Floriańska down ul. Grodzka to the castle-cathedral complex atop Wawel, was another one of those battlefields, one rich in symbolism.

The Kraków Main Square is one of the great public spaces in the world, not simply for its size (650 feet by 650 feet) but for the splendor of the buildings that compose its perimeter, the noble structures within it, and the palpable sense the *Rynek* conveys that *here* is one of the great crossroads of Europe, indeed of Western civilization: a place of conversation and debate; a place of trade and commerce; a place of encounter between peoples, cultures, and languages. For centuries, the Main Square was also the site of one of Kraków's great

Sukiennice (Drapers' Hall)

religious events, the Corpus Christi (or, as it's known in Polish, Corpus Domini) procession. Every year, on the Thursday after Trinity Sunday, the archbishop of Kraków would lead a great public procession in honor of the Holy Eucharist, departing from **Wawel,** walking up the Royal Mile into the *Rynek,* and then processing the Blessed Sacrament, reserved in an ancient gold monstrance, around the square. Four altars were erected in the *Rynek Główny,* one on each of its sides. At each of these altars, the procession would pause, the Blessed Sacrament would be reposed in honor, and the archbishop of Kraków would deliver a sermon. The procession finally returned to Wawel, where the Blessed Sacrament would be honored again with prayer, song, and incense.

This ancient public manifestation of Catholic faith in the eucharistic Body and Blood of Christ was banned by the Nazi governor-general Hans Frank throughout the Second

World War. During Poland's communist period, the struggle to restore the Corpus Christi procession was a focal point of the contest in Kraków between the Catholic Church and the Communist Party—between the Polish people and their traditions, and those determined to erase those traditions. At first, the local communist authorities only permitted a severely truncated procession: the archbishop, carrying the gold monstrance, would leave **Wawel Cathedral,** turn left, enter the palace precincts under the portal with the Latin inscription SI DEUS NOBISCUM QUIS CONTRA NOS (If God is with us, who can be against us), and process with the Blessed Sacrament around the courtyard of the **Royal Castle**—a procedure that effectively put the Corpus Christi procession under a form of house arrest and drastically reduced the number of Cracovians able to participate.

Relentless pressure on the authorities from Karol Wojtyła during his years as archbishop of Kraków finally led to a slight but significant easing of the restrictions on Kraków's Corpus Christi procession. The *Rynek Główny* was still under the ban, in a communist version of what Richard John Neuhaus would call the "naked public square"—a public space shorn of religious conviction and transcendent moral reference points. But some concessions were made. The procession was allowed to leave Wawel Hill and walk two blocks up ul. Grodzka before turning left at ul. Poselska and continuing back to Wawel along two blocks of ul. Straszewski. Along this truncated route, the traditional four altars were erected. And at those altars, during the 1970s, Karol Wojtyła emerged as a charismatic public speaker and leader, a man with the wit, courage, and rhetorical skills to summon his people to reclaim and live the truth about themselves, which included the truth of their Catholic faith.

DESPITE HIS TRAINING in the theater, Wojtyła was not a man naturally given to raising his voice; he was far more the scholar-poet than the rhetorician, and he never played the demagogue (indeed, in his play *Our God's Brother,* he painted a striking portrait of demagoguery and its distortion of freedom in the character of the Stranger, a kind of crypto-Lenin). But his responsibilities as archbishop of Kraków, and thus *defensor civitatis,* required that he grow from being an intriguing if challenging preacher, addressing hundreds of congregants within the confines of a church, to being a commanding public personality, addressing tens of thousands of people from every walk of life, typically outdoors. So that is what he did, in sermons and addresses at a variety of Polish shrines, such as the Marian shrine at Piekary Śląskie, which annually attracted hundreds of thousands of miners to a day-long men's pilgrimage in which grandfathers walked with their sons and grandsons, the adults in the colorful uniforms of the miners' guilds. And that is also what he did in the reconstituted Corpus Christi procession: he became the man who could, on October 22, 1978, challenge the Church and the world to fearlessness—"Be not afraid!"—and to the adventure of faith: "Open the doors to Christ!"

Thus on June 10, 1971, the first year the Corpus Christi procession was permitted to leave Wawel and enter the Old Town, Cardinal Wojtyła used his sermon at the fourth altar to make a bold defense of his people's Catholic and Christian identity, in the face of communist efforts to redefine what it meant to be Polish and to enforce that redefinition by coercive state power: "We are the citizens of our country, the citizens of our city, but we are also a people of God which has its own Christian sensibility. . . . We will continue to demand our rights. They are obvious, just as our presence here is obvious. We will demand!"

The next year, preaching at the first stational altar atop Wawel, the archbishop described the Corpus Christi procession as an expression of something essential to being Cracovian: what they were about to begin, he told his people, was more than a religious observance of interest to a few; it was "a procession . . . of our city, of our whole history." He drove home the same message two years later, crying out at the 1974 Corpus Christi procession, "We are not from the periphery!" after which he bluntly denounced the state's refusal to grant permission for building new churches, such that citizens of Poland had to "stand for years on end under the open sky" to exercise the religious freedom guaranteed by their constitution—"What program is that part of?"

The communist authorities doubtless thought that this archbishop, whom they had imagined in the early 1960s as a mixture of dreamy poet and theoretical academic, was playing politics. And, in a sense, he was. But it was politics understood as an extension of ethics, and ethics rooted in religious conviction. So during the 1977 Corpus Christi procession, after warning the Communist Party and state at the first stational altar that the demand for public acknowledgment of basic human rights was growing throughout the world and could not be denied, he drew the connection between challenging abusive totalitarian power and the Catholic faith of his people in these striking terms, preaching at the fourth stational altar: "I ask forgiveness from Our Lord that—at least seemingly—I did not speak of Him. But it only seems that way. I spoke of our matters . . . so that we might all understand that He, living in the sacrament of the Eucharist, lives our human life."

All Catholics are baptized into the three "missions" of Christ: the missions of prophet, priest, and king, which are missions to speak the truth, to worship in truth, and to serve others in truth. Catholics in Holy Orders are ordained to live that triple mission in a unique way, one that empowers all the people of God in the Body of Christ to be the disciples in mission they were commissioned to be at their baptism. Karol Wojtyła embodied that threefold mission in a dramatic, powerful way during the Kraków Corpus Christi processions. He spoke truth, and spoke truth to power, without reservation but always inviting conversion. He carried the eucharistic Christ, the great high priest who feeds his people with the bread of life, giving them strength and courage for the arduous journey of fidelity and resistance. And in doing these things, he was the servant of all, enabling others to be servants in a land in which power was misconstrued as brute force and from which solidarity had been banished.

PHOTOGRAPHS OF THESE processions in the 1970s, taken from the rooftops of the Old Town or from atop Wawel, show tens of thousands, even hundreds of thousands, of Cracovians jamming the streets of the Old Town in a massive display of resistance to the communist authorities—and to the untruths about Poland and Poles that were an essential component of the communist program. Led by Karol Wojtyła, the Kraków Corpus Christi procession became a defense of the human rights of all, believers and unbelievers, such that the Royal Mile, or those portions of it the procession was allowed to traverse, became an itinerary of liberation for everyone. The Body of Christ, the Church, defended the rights of all (and not just its own prerogatives) because it had been nourished in the Holy Eucharist by the Body and Blood of Christ, who came that all "might have life, and have it to the full" (John 10:10).

The breadth of the Church's concerns for the dignity and rights of all was mirrored in the spaciousness of the *Rynek Główny*—even if the Corpus Christi procession was not allowed to enter the square. That experience of openness, of depth and width and height, is sometimes difficult to see from outside the Church. From outside, the Church (especially as caricatured by its enemies) can seem small and dark, cramped and confining. That is not how mature Catholics experience the Church, however. Experienced from inside, Catholicism is remarkably spacious and open, a place of light and color—attributes perhaps best captured in the experience of the great Gothic cathedrals with their high naves and stunning stained glass.

Preaching in one of those cathedrals, St. Patrick's in New York, during his 2008 pilgrimage to the United States, Pope Benedict XVI used his surroundings to underscore the openness and luminosity of the Church, and how that brilliance calls the Church into mission:

I would like to draw your attention to a few aspects of this beautiful structure, which I think can serve as a starting point for a reflection on . . . the Mystical Body.

The first has to do with the stained glass windows, which flood the interior with mystic light. From the outside, those windows are dark, heavy, even dreary. But once one enters the church, they come alive; reflecting the light passing through them, they reveal all their splendor. Many writers—here in America we can think of Nathaniel Hawthorne—have used the image of stained glass to illustrate the mystery of the Church herself. It is only from the inside, from the experience of faith and ecclesial life, that we see the Church as she truly is: flooded with grace, resplendent in beauty, adorned by the manifold gifts of the Spirit. It follows that we, who live the life of grace within the Church's communion, are called to draw all people into this mystery of light. . . .

The unity of a Gothic cathedral, as we know, is not the static unity of a classical temple, but a unity born of the dynamic tension of diverse forces which impel the architecture upward, pointing it to heaven. Here, too, we can see a symbol of the Church's unity, which is the unity—as St. Paul has told us—of a living body composed of many different members, each with its own role and purpose. . . .

So let us lift our gaze upward! And with great humility and confidence, let us ask the Spirit to enable us each day to grow in the holiness that will make us living stones in the temple which he is even now raising in the midst of our world.

The English novelist Evelyn Waugh made the same point in a similar way in a book written by Catholic converts like himself, shortly after World War II: "Come inside," Waugh suggested. The extraordinary expansiveness of Catholicism—its capacity to absorb and refine elements of a vast variety of cultures, its openness to the entirety of the human condition—can only be discerned, and appreciated, from inside, just as the exceptional lightness and openness of the Kraków Main Square has to be experienced in person to be fully appreciated.

ONE OF THE most prominent features of the Kraków Main Square is the **Basilica of the Assumption of Our Lady,** known to one and all as the *Mariacki*. At the end of the communist period, the *Mariacki* was dark and blackened: its brick exterior, its roof, its stained glass. Today, the *Mariacki* is a radiant mix

*Basilica of the Assumption of Our Lady (*Mariacki*)*

of red brick, bronze-colored copper, and spectacular stained glass. Even the most casual visitors are immediately struck by its polychromed ceiling, with gold stars shining from a deep blue background, and by the extraordinary carved wood altarpiece by the Nuremberg artist Wit Stwosz (stolen by the Nazis during the war and now restored to its proper setting). To the right of the sanctuary, however, is an important feature of the *Mariacki* that the casual visitor may inadvertently miss, but which the pilgrim will not: the confessional in which Father Karol Wojtyła sat daily, from 1951 until 1958, reconciling men and women to God and offering them courage to continue on the journey of a Christian life.

Decades later, the priest who sat in that confessional, now become Pope John Paul II, would write an exhortation to the world Church, *Reconciliatio et Paenitentia* (Reconciliation and Penance), in which he described the confession of sins as an exercise in a true, Christian humanism. Getting it wrong— that is, sinning—is, John Paul wrote, "an integral part of the truth about man," and to deny that is to truncate freedom— rather like the way the communist authorities tried to truncate the Corpus Christi procession. To take sin seriously is to take freedom seriously, and to take the drama of the moral life—life "in the gap" between the person I am and the person I ought to be—seriously.

Thus confessionals, like the confessional Wojtyła used in the *Mariacki,* are arenas in which the Church recognizes the full, personal, and dramatic character of the human condition. Here confessor and penitent, in what John Paul called "one of the most awe-inspiring innovations of the Gospel," deepen the experience of freedom and responsibility that is a defining

Father Karol Wojtyła's confessional, Basilica of the Assumption of Our Lady (Mariacki)

characteristic of human maturity, and do so in a uniquely sacramental way: God, the father of mercies, through the Church and her priest, restores the squandered dignity of wayward sons and daughters, clothing them again with the robes of beloved children and calling them to a celebratory feast, as in the gospel account of the Prodigal Son (Luke 15:11–32).

Father Karol Wojtyła was a "fantastic confessor," according to one of his friends and penitents, uninterested in the "mass production of Christians" in a confessional assembly line, but deeply committed to accompanying a fellow believer in his or her quest for the truth, including the truth of failure and the truth about making wise decisions. Yet Wojtyła, the confessor who gently prodded good decisions, never imposed decisions. "*You* must decide" was his signature phrase in spiritual direction. One couldn't opt out of the drama of life in the gap. One had to decide—and, with the grace of God and the support of the Church, wise and true decisions could be made.

Pondering Wojtyła's confessional, and Wojtyła in that confessional as confessor, confidant, and spiritual director, the pilgrim in the *Mariacki* may gain new insight into the Catholic concept of the priest as one who acts *in persona Christi* (in the person of Christ) by reflecting on the foundation of this sacramental ministry, which Father Wojtyła once described to some of his young friends during a student retreat in 1954: "One man experienced the might of the holiness of God: Jesus Christ. He bore the weight of man's guilt and stood bearing this ballast before God. The awareness of sin on the one hand and of the holiness of God on the other drew him to sacrifice himself and to union with God. This explains the mystery of the garden of Gethsemane and of Golgotha."

The Main Market Square and the Royal Mile

From the Planty, the great greensward that surrounds the Kraków Old Town, all roads lead to the center of the old city: the *Rynek Główny*, or Main Market Square. What Wawel Hill is to the Polish nobility and the Jagiellonian University is to Polish academics, the *Rynek Główny* is to Kraków's burgher class, the lively and enterprising souls who made Kraków a crossroads of commerce and politics, a place for entertainment, news gathering, and news sharing: activities that have been going on in the square for centuries, and which continue day and night today, in what has become a truly global space.

The construction of the *Rynek Główny* was one of the ambitious projects that followed the city's being granted "Magdeburg Rights"—a civic constitution based on the medieval corporate law first established in the German city of Magdeburg—in 1257. Among other things, the charter shifted the city center to the north and west, away from what is now the *Plac Dominikanów* and ul. Stolarska (which passes by the *Mały Rynek,* the Little Square) to the vast Main Square known today.

The perimeter of the *Rynek* is largely composed of brightly colored, four- and five-story magnate homes, once the Cracovian residences of some of Poland's greatest noble families; today, their ground floors are home to restaurants, cafes, and shops, while the upper stories are used as offices and apartments. The long, rectangular *Sukiennice,* the Cloth Hall or Drapers' Hall at the center of the square, now houses ground-level craft shops, an underground museum exploring the archaeology of Kraków, and a second-story art museum, which includes several important historical paintings by Jan Matejko, rector of the Kraków Academy of Fine Arts, whose home, now a museum, is at Floriańska 41 in the Old Town, north of the *Rynek*. To the southwest of the *Sukiennice* is a massive brick and stone fire tower, all that remains of the old city hall. The tiny chapel of St. Adalbert (St. Wojciech) is sited at an angle in the southeast corner of the square.

The northeast corner of the *Rynek Główny* is defined by the vast brick and copper-roofed **Basilica of the Assumption of Our Lady,** the *Mariacki,* whose asymmetrical crowned towers can be seen from all over Kraków. The basilica predates the *Rynek*—its origins can be traced to 1222—and thus the basilica does not conform to the geometric symmetry of the rest of the square.

The *Mariacki* is also home to one of Kraków's most distinctive traditions, the hourly sounding of the *Hejnal,* a foreshortened trumpet call, every hour on the hour, to north, south, east, and west. Because of their height, the basilica's towers were long used as watchtowers, the watchmen (who would sound the alarm by bugle) on the alert for fire or marauders. The *Hejnal* honors the memory of the watchful bugler who, while warning the city of an impending invasion in 1241, was struck in the throat by a Mongol arrow in midnote. Thus the *Hejnal,* which was the aural signature of the BBC's Polish service during World War II, stops abruptly in midnote.

After the death of Pope John Paul II, a new tradition of trumpeting from the *Mariacki* was created. Each first Saturday of the month, at the precise moment of the Pope's death (9:37 p.m. Central European Time), the *Mariacki* trumpeter sounds a Polish hymn in honor of Poland's most distinguished son.

Sukiennice
Rynek Główny

The *Sukiennice,* built as a center for trade at the height of the city's grandeur, might be considered the world's oldest shopping mall.

What began as informal market stalls where merchants sold their goods was transformed into a Gothic-style hall in the mid-fourteenth century. A hundred years later, the Cloth Hall or Drapers' Hall was renovated in Renaissance style. Further renovations in the 1870s incorporated elements of Gothic and Renaissance design, both visible today. Its location at the very center of the *Rynek Główny* seems to have protected the *Sukiennice* from the citywide fires that demolished other parts of Kraków with disturbing frequency.

When the newly renovated *Sukiennice* reopened in 1879, Poles from all three partitioned parts of the country participated. During a ceremonial ball marking the reopening, the artist Henryk Siemiradzki announced his decision to give the city his painting "Nero's Torches" as the founding piece for a new national museum, the Sukiennice Museum. His generosity began a collection now largely composed of historical and patriotic paintings emphasizing the continuity of Polish culture and identity despite the loss of national independence. By the 1930s, the Sukiennice Museum's collections boasted an inventory of three hundred thousand pieces.

The museum was closed during the twentieth-century world wars but escaped serious damage and was reopened at each war's end. Between 2006 and 2010, the Sukiennice Museum, now part of the National Museum of Kraków, underwent further renovations, upgrading its technology and improving its thematic layout. Today, the original donation, "Nero's Torches" by Henryk Siemiradzki, is still displayed, as are Jan Matejko's "Prussian Homage" and late baroque, rococo, and neoclassicist pieces depicting historic scenes from Poland's stormy past.

The Basilica of the Assumption of Our Lady: The *Mariacki*
Rynek Główny

The great Gothic structure universally known as the *Mariacki* is located at what seems, at first glance, an odd angle within the symmetrical lines of the Main Market Square—an angle that underscores the basilica's unique place in the hearts of all Cracovians and many Poles. The original church in the site was destroyed during the Mongol invasion of 1241, and a new church, in the early Gothic style, was built in 1290–1300. Fifty years later, King Kazimierz the Great had the church completely rebuilt; some of the funding was provided by the magnate Mikołaj Wierzynek, whose home, now an eponymous restaurant, was on the south side of the *Rynek Główny*. During Kazimierz's renovation, the *Mariacki's* vaults were reworked; tall, slender windows were installed; and the presbytery or sanctuary was extended.

Many of the side chapels were added in the fifteenth century, and the crowned Gothic north tower was raised to facilitate its use as a watchtower. The second, southern tower, which houses five bells, did not reach its current height or form until 1592.

The most famous piece of art inside the *Mariacki* is the carved wooden altarpiece, the work of Wit Stwosz (Veit Stoss) of Nuremberg, who at the time was considered Europe's greatest sculptor. The late Gothic panels, crafted in 1473, depict the Assumption of Mary into heaven (the fourth Glorious Mystery of the rosary), and her coronation as queen of heaven and earth (the fifth Glorious Mystery), as witnessed by Sts. Adalbert (Wojciech) and Stanisław; the composition also includes numerous scenes from the Bible, with local Cracovians serving as Stwosz's model for biblical figures—a reflection of both the unity of the Old and New Testaments and what the creeds call the "Communion of Saints." Stolen by the occupying Nazis during World War II and taken back to Nuremberg (where Wit Stwosz is buried), this masterpiece was recovered after the war and replaced in the church in 1957, after years of restoration.

Another of Wit Stwosz's masterworks, a crucifix carved in 1491 from a single block of stone and known as the Slacker (from Henryk Slacker, who commissioned it), may be found to the right of the sanctuary, near the side chapel and confessional where Father Karol Wojtyła exercised his ministry as a confessor between 1951 and 1958.

Choir loft, Basilica of the Assumption of Our Lady (Mariacki)

The interior of the basilica was renovated once again in the eighteenth century by artist and sculptor Francesco Placidi, who brought a late baroque style to the *Mariacki*. Many of the church's distinctive polychrome walls were the work of Andrzej Radwański.

In 1795, when Kraków was under Austrian rule, the authorities made an effort to improve the city's sanitary standards, in the course of which the cemetery in the old churchyard was demolished and replaced by a new square, *Plac Mariacki* (Marian Square).

The blue and gold ceilings of today's *Mariacki*, complemented with rich reds in a neo-Gothic style, were designed by Tadeusz Stryjeński, who undertook yet another renovation of the church in 1887–1891, likely as a result of the great fire of 1850. The most notable of Polish historical painters, Jan Matejko, designed, painted, and funded many of the new interior murals. Matejko's designs can also be seen in some of the stained glass windows, which were executed by his great students Stanisław Wyspiański and Józef Mehoffer, both of whom also made major contributions to the Franciscan basilica in the Old Town.

When Mehmet Ali Agca shot John Paul II in St. Peter's Square on May 13, 1981, half a million Poles, dressed in white, processed from the Kraków Commons (the ***Błonia Krakowskie***) to the *Rynek Główny*, where Karol Wojtyła's successor as archbishop of Kraków, Cardinal Franciszek Macharski, celebrated a Mass for the recovery of the gravely wounded Pope in front of the *Mariacki*: a celebration replicated by John Paul II himself, in different circumstances, during the 1991 papal pilgrimage to Poland.

The most recent addition to the *Mariacki* is a great bronze sculpture in a niche in the rear of the church, on the north side of the exterior, commissioned for the Great Jubilee of 2000. The saints of Kraków's millennium-long history of faith and witness are depicted with the Blessed Virgin Mary and St. John beneath the Cross of Christ: St. Jan Kanty, St. Maximilian Kolbe, St. Jadwiga, St. Stanisław, St. Maria Faustina Kowalska, St. Albert Chmielowski (*Brat Albert,* the "brother of our God" in Karol Wojtyła's play, a onetime Polish freedom fighter turned avant-garde painter turned consecrated religious brother and servant of the poorest of the poor), and St. Rafał Kalinowski (another veteran of the 1863 Polish rebellion, who subsequently entered the Carmelites). [C.G.]

Nowa Huta and the Ark Church

The Universal Call to Holiness

The epic struggle to build a Catholic church in Nowa Huta, a challenge to the communist determination that this model "workers' town" would be the first in Polish history without a place of worship, was one of the defining elements of Karol Wojtyła's stewardship of the archdiocese of Kraków. The battle for God and for human dignity in Nowa Huta also embodied, in a singularly dramatic way, many of the chief themes of Wojtyła's episcopate, which would be replicated on a global scale in the pontificate of John Paul II: religious freedom in full as the first of human rights; the universal call to holiness; the Eucharist as the source and center of the Church's life; and the defense of the family.

NOWA HUTA WAS a colossal, and ultimately futile, attempt to create New Soviet Man in Poland: the *robotnik*, the worker, who lived the Marxist-Leninist dream of the dictatorship of the proletariat; the reconstituted human being who had thrown off the shackles placed on humanity by the God of the Bible. The "atheistic humanism" analyzed by Wojtyła's friend

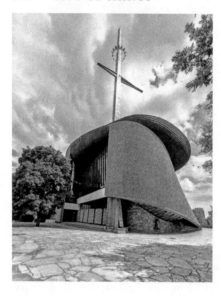

Ark Church

Henri de Lubac was no string of philosophical abstractions in Nowa Huta; it was a social program, an economic program, a political program, and, in the final analysis, an anthropological program—a project dedicated to nothing less than the remaking of the human condition.

In its first phases, Nowa Huta was a deliberate attempt to undermine the traditional Catholic culture of what remained, in the years immediately following World War II, a largely rural country. Recruiters sought to entice young Poles, men and women, to leave their country homes and "build socialism" in Nowa Huta—while at the same time abandoning the culture and morals of their past in a new town where there would be no priests, no nuns, and no parents to remind them of Catholic sexual ethics. A generation before the Sixties hit San Francisco and New York, the idea of "free love" was promoted in Nowa Huta as part and parcel of the communist project of remaking Poles in the image and likeness of Marx, Lenin, Stalin, and their obsessions.

Later, when the ideological fever of postwar Polish Stalinism cooled and the Polish state hardened into a clotted, bureaucratic, power-obsessed, and paranoid kind of mafia enterprise, Nowa Huta continued to be developed as a town devoid of human solidarity and traditional Polish family life. Its buildings were dull expressions of socialist-functionalist architecture, and the crude sculpture that decorated the public spaces gave socialist realism an even worse name than it had already acquired, at least among those with any aesthetic sense. The flats in the great apartment blocks in Nowa Huta were kept deliberately small, discouraging large families. Work schedules in the steel mills and their supporting shops were arranged so that parents had little time with each other and little time together with their children, who were consigned to the care of state-run nurseries and schools. There was no access from one flat to another along the long axis of apartment blocks that amounted to human filing cabinets: to visit the adjacent apartment, one had to go down to the ground floor, exit the building, and go in by another entrance—thus facilitating the work of secret police surveillance. Special stores catered to the consumer desires of Communist Party members, underscoring the distinction between "true" citizens and others. Everything about Nowa Huta was an attempt to nullify what in the West would be called "civil society"; the authorities bent every effort toward atomizing the population and preventing the planting of those free, voluntary associations that are the sinews and ligaments of a free society.

The rewriting of history was also part of the communist project at Nowa Huta. The careful reconstruction of the Kraków Old Town in the mid-nineteenth century, done after the catastrophic citywide fire of 1850, and the Old Town's multiple architectural schemes and rich decoration embodied in stone and brick the heroic national "story" by which Poland lived during the years when it had lost its political independence. The heavy industry and strictly functional architecture of Nowa Huta deliberately told a different story: the new mythology of the dictatorship of the proletariat in the utopia of the workers' state. And over time, even as the Nowa Huta story failed to seize the imaginations of those in whose name it was putatively constructed, the new town itself began to eat away at old Kraków—literally, as the polluted air and microscopic shards of steel belching from Nowa Huta's mills began to destroy the fabric of the Old Town.

The challenge in Nowa Huta, then, was more than the challenge of building a church in the face of communist authorities determined to enforce a naked public square. The struggle for a solid, palpable Catholic presence in the town-without-God was a struggle for the dignity of the human person, a struggle for the dignity of the family, a struggle for solidarity, and a struggle for the meaning of "Poland."

THE PEOPLE OF Nowa Huta declined, in the main, to follow the script that communist ideology had written for them. For years, the people erected a cross on an empty field in the new town as a reminder of the church they hoped would be built there one day; the communist authorities would bulldoze the cross, which would be replaced within a matter of days. On December 24, 1959, the auxiliary bishop of Kraków, Karol Wojtyła, who knew precisely what the communist game was in Nowa Huta, began celebrating an open-air Christmas midnight Mass in the model workers' town, at the site where the people intended the church to be built; thousands attended, often in deep snow and always in freezing weather.

Wojtyła the philosopher understood the Church's contest with communism at its deepest level: as a battle between radically different ideas of the human person, human community, human origins, and human destiny. In addition, the contest with communism was a battle for the very meaning of history. Communism, following Marx's form of atheistic humanism, contended that history was the exhaust fumes of the means of production, or impersonal economic processes; when the proletariat controlled the means of production (tutored by the "vanguard" Bolshevik Party, in Lenin's addition to communist orthodoxy), all would be well and history would resolve itself in an ultramundane heaven on earth. Karol Wojtyła, for his part, thought that the most dynamic force in history was culture, and at the center of culture was the human person—the full truth of whose incomparable worth and inalienable dignity had been revealed in Jesus Christ. Thus to contend for religious freedom in Nowa Huta was far, far more than a matter of the Church flexing its institutional muscle; it was a matter of the truth about the human person in full. Or as Wojtyła's longtime secretary, Stanisław Dziwisz, would write decades later: "The Nowa Huta experience permanently shaped Wojtyła's pastoral program as an archbishop, just as it permanently shaped [his] personality as

Sanctuary, Ark Church

an unyielding defender of human rights, of the rights of freedom of conscience and religion." The archbishop of Kraków
would eventually take that message to the world, as Bishop
of Rome. But as Dziwisz noted, with precision, John Paul II's
battle "on behalf of the dignity of the human person began
right there at Nowa Huta."

WOJTYŁA WON THE battle for Nowa Huta and, on May 15,
1977, consecrated the *Matki Bożej Królowej Polski—Arka Pana*
(the **Ark of Our Lord and of Our Lady, Queen of Poland**) in
the center of Nowa Huta—a strikingly modern church, intended to evoke images of Noah's ark and the barque of the
Church, where the People of God gathered to ride through
the rough seas and stormy winds of history, under the banner

of the Cross (the ark's mast) and the protection of Mary. Known locally as the *Arka,* the facade of the first church in Nowa Huta—composed of two million polished stones from the riverbeds of Poland—deliberately links the present to the past in a reaffirmation of the history that communism tried to rewrite. So does the great sculpture of the Crucified One that hovers over the *Arka's* sanctuary: forged by the workers at the Nowa Huta steel mills, its dramatic composition affirmed the truths about the human person, about God, and about God's relationship to his human creation that communism flatly denied. So does the great icon of the Black Madonna in the sanctuary. Even the tabernacle teaches a lesson: against the communist notion of nature as cosmic accident, the *Arka* tabernacle, which includes a piece of moon rock given to Pope Paul VI by American astronauts, speaks of the cosmic Christ, present to his people today in the Holy Eucharist, in whose life, death, and resurrection both nature and history are redeemed and restored to the trajectory intended by the Creator.

Cardinal Wojtyła's homily at the consecration Mass drew together in one vivid tapestry the many threads of truth that had been woven together in the struggle for the church in Nowa Huta—including the truth that this house of worship and prayer, this repository of the Eucharistic Christ, had been made possible by innumerable acts of sacrifice and fidelity:

> We want this temple, which has a Mother as its patroness, to be our mother. We also want this temple, whose patroness is the Queen of Poland, to reign over us. Most of all, however, we long for the Mother. We feel such a strong need for her presence at this turn in

history where mankind now finds itself, where Europe and our homeland find themselves. . . .

This city is not a city of people who belong to no one. Of people, to whom one may do whatever one wants, who may be manipulated according to the laws or rules of production and consumption. This is a city of the children of God [and] this temple was needed so that this could be expressed, [so] that it could be emphasized. . . .

We still have among us those . . . who began to build [this church] with their suffering. We pay them the highest respect. . . . Was it not possible—is it still not possible—to take another path as we continue to struggle to build other houses of God which are so necessary in Poland? . . .

Let us hope that in our homeland, which has a Christian and humanitarian past, these two orders— light and the Gospel, and respect for human rights— come together more effectively in the future.

A week and a half after consecrating the *Arka*, Cardinal Wojtyła met with a group of priests he had ordained in 1974. There he drew another, deeply personal lesson from the battle that had just been victoriously concluded in Nowa Huta, reflecting on what he often heard from young men about the reason why they entered the seminary:

And often . . . I hear . . . that it was these times, times of great struggle between good and evil, times of great struggle between Mary and Satan, that draw many . . .

into the priesthood, so that they might participate in this great battle fully, decisively, in a defined manner. . . . [Yet] this battle runs through the heart of each of us.

HOW CAN CHRISTIANS be nourished and strengthened to fight the primordial battle, which occurs along the fault line that runs through every human heart? Prayer, certainly; the sacrament of Reconciliation or Penance, without a doubt. But above all, in Karol Wojtyła's view of the spiritual life, courage and power to fight for what is right, and for the dignity of the human person and the family, come from the Holy Eucharist. That is why it would have been completely insufficient to have anything other than a great church in Nowa Huta: a place where the Catholic community could celebrate sacramentally Christ's presence in his body and blood; a place where the Catholic community could join its sacrifices and struggles to the sacramental representation of the sacrifice of the Cross; a place where food for the journey could be sought, and found.

It would be a mistake, then, to treat the *Arka* as the symbol of a political triumph. It certainly marked a way station on the Polish road to freedom, but it was, and is, a distinctive kind of station: it is a temple, a tabernacle, where the People of God fully experience themselves as the mystical Body of Christ, by receiving Christ's body and blood under the forms of bread and wine, and by worshipping his Eucharistic presence in the reserved Blessed Sacrament.

As he prepared to mark the silver jubilee of his pontificate, the bishop who was unbending in his determination that the Eucharist would be celebrated and reverenced in a church in Nowa Huta shared what he called his "Eucharistic amazement" with the entire Church as Bishop of Rome, in the encyclical letter *Ecclesia de Eucharistia* (The Church from the Eucharist). Issued on April 17, 2003, as Catholics around the world entered the most sacred time of the year and began the Paschal Triduum of Holy Thursday, Good Friday, and the Easter Vigil, John Paul II lifted up in his last encyclical the extraordinary reality of the Eucharist as Catholics understand it: "In this gift, Jesus Christ entrusted to his Church the perennial making present of the paschal mystery . . . and brought about the mysterious 'oneness in time' between the Triduum and the passage of the centuries." The Eucharist thus gives new and deeper meaning to history: for the Eucharist has a "truly enormous 'capacity' [that] embraces all of history as the recipient of the grace of the redemption."

The Eucharist is also, in a sense, cosmic—another theme that links the *Arka* of Nowa Huta to the mature teaching of John Paul II:

Even when it is celebrated on the humble altar of a country church, the Eucharist is always in some way celebrated on the altar of the world. It unites heaven and earth. It embraces and permeates all creation. The Son of God became man in order to restore all creation, in one supreme act of praise, to the One who made it from nothing. He, the Eternal High Priest who by the blood of his Cross entered the eternal sanctuary, thus gives back to the Creator and Father all creation redeemed. He does so through the priestly ministry of the Church, to the glory of the Most Holy Trinity. Truly this is the *mysterium fidei* [mystery of faith] which is accomplished in the Eucharist: the world which came forth from the hands of God the Creator now returns to him redeemed by Christ.

Nourished by the Eucharist, the people of the Church are empowered to answer what the Second Vatican Council described as the "universal call to holiness"—a theme that Karol Wojtyła preached throughout more than fifty-eight years as priest and bishop. Holiness is not for the sanctuary alone. Holiness is not for religious "professionals"—the ordained and those in consecrated religious life—alone. Holiness is every Christian's baptismal calling. And because baptism sacramentally confers the grace of divine life that God had offered humanity in the beginning, holiness is every Christian's *human* destiny and calling. To be the men and women we are meant to be—to narrow that gap between the person I am and the person I ought to be—is to grow in holiness.

Holiness is the ultimate meaning of human dignity, and the true meaning of human destiny. That is the truth over which the battle for Nowa Huta was fought. That is the truth that the celebration and reservation of the Holy Eucharist in the *Arka Pana* of Nowa Huta continues to teach the world.

Nowa Huta

Kraków was a thorn in the side of Poland's communist authorities from the end of the Second World War to the Revolution of 1989. Having voted "incorrectly" in the bogus "people's referendum" of 1946 and the equally rigged "parliamentary election" of 1947, Kraków was punished by having Nowa Huta located on the city's eastern outskirts—a built-from-scratch steel-milling town that would, by its very existence, draw a sharp (and, it was hoped, educational) contrast to Kraków, the city of royalty, Kraków the city of scholarship and art, Kraków the commercial crossroads—and Kraków, the spiritual heart of Poland. That the location of Nowa Huta was ill-suited to steel manufacture (raw materials had to be hauled in from distant regions) made no difference: the point was to make an ideological point.

The construction of Nova Huta ("New Mill" in Polish) began in 1949, and from the outset, the city plan (which included wide boulevards for May Day parades) included no church—a first in the millennium-long history of Poland. At the height of production in the 1970s, Nova Huta produced 6.7 million tons of steel per year. What it did not produce was "New Soviet Man," Polish-style. The people of Nowa Huta demanded a church, and made that demand known by erecting a large wooden cross on the site where they thought a parish church should be built. Bulldozed and rebuilt, time after time, the Nowa Huta cross became a powerful symbol of the failure of the communist program of remaking Poles in the image and likeness of proper communist workers.

Years of resistance led by Archbishop Karol Wojtyła were rewarded when, in 1967, permission was finally given to build a church in Nowa Huta. The project, done entirely by volunteer labor and supported by contributions from all over Europe, took a decade to complete. The church was dedicated on

May 15, 1977, in a driving rainstorm to which none of the tens of thousands present paid the slightest attention.

The Ark Church (Ark of Our Lord and of Our Lady, Queen of Poland)
ul. Obrońców Krzyża, 1
Nowa Huta

Designed by Wojciech Pietrzyk, the Ark Church is a striking architectural metaphor: the people of the Church, gathered in a boat reminiscent of Noah's ark and the fishing craft sailed by the apostles on the Sea of Galilee, are carried through the tem-

Ark Church

pests of history, led by the Cross (the roof-boat's 230-foot-tall mast) and protected by the prayers of the Mother of God, the Queen of Poland. In addition to its deliberate biblical form, the *Arka*'s fluid lines, rounded edges, and asymmetry stand in stark contrast to Nowa Huta's architectural angularity and rigid street grids.

The interior is dominated by a twenty-seven-foot-tall steel figure of the crucified Christ, designed by Bronisław Chromy and forged by the workers in the Nowa Huta mills, which soars over the sanctuary. A large icon of the Black Madonna is the companion piece on the opposite side of the freestanding altar. Beneath the figure of Christ is a tabernacle in the form of a globe; embedded in it is a fragment of rock from the moon, given to the church by Pope Paul VI (who received it from American astronauts and who also gave the church a stone from the tomb of St. Peter). Contemporary stained glass windows evoke biblical memories of the rainbow that followed the Flood.

The basement floor of the *Arka* includes a chapel dedicated to Our Lady of Fatima, where the Blessed Sacrament is exposed for adoration. The chapel contains numerous *votum* gifts offered in thanksgiving for graces received and a small statue of St. John Paul II.

Among the church's treasures is a statue dedicated to "Our Lady of the Armored" (*Matki Bożej Pancernej*)—a one-and-a-half-foot-tall sculpture composed of shrapnel removed from Polish soldiers wounded at the Battle of Monte Cassino in World War II.

In the early 1980s, and especially after the declaration of martial law in December 1981, the Ark Church became a focal point of anti-communist protests and a stronghold of the Soli-

Bogdan Włosik Memorial,
Nowa Huta

darity movement. A stone memorial across the street from the church entrance commemorates the sacrifice of Bogdan Włosik, a young man shot during a demonstration against martial law.

In September 2012, the Kraków City Council awarded the *Arka* the *Cracoviae Merenti,* a silver medal acknowledging the church's significance to the city's history. [C.G.]

Kalwaria Zebrzydowska and Tyniec

Prayer, Contemplation,
and Living Biblically

"Pastoral planning" is a staple of twenty-first-century Catholic life in parishes and diocesan offices. In a sense, pastoral planning is as old as St. Paul's missionary journeys, during which the apostle, through a letter, informed a young Christian community of his plans to continue his work—calling men and women to conversion and forming new Christians in the Gospel way of life—with the recipient community or in some new place. In the contemporary sense of the term, pastoral planning usually refers to church management, with responsible clergy and laity fitting resources to programs in a rational, orderly process.

In his years as archbishop of Kraków, Karol Wojtyła had a distinctive approach to pastoral planning. Taking counsel with his associates about an opportunity to be seized or a problem to be addressed, his first question was "What is the truth of the Gospel that sheds light on this question?" And the second was "Whom do we have—or whom can we train—to help?" The second question reflected Wojtyła's remarkable openness to a wide range of expertise and his complete lack

Benedictine Abbey at Tyniec

of clericalism. But the first question, the Gospel question, was decisive. Pastoral planning, as Karol Wojtyła understood it, was not a subset of management theory; it was a kind of practical theology, a matter of seeing the world through Gospel lenses, seeing his local Church as a shepherd sees his flock, and laying plans accordingly.

The extensive pastoral program that Wojtyła implemented in Kraków, and his own key decisions in shaping that program, were products of both consultation and prayer. Most leaders make decisions at their desks or around a conference table. Karol Wojtyła made his most important decisions on his knees, or walking in silent prayer and contemplation at special places that lent themselves to that kind of reflecting and deciding.

Two of those places, to which he frequently repaired during his decade and a half at the helm of the Church of Kraków, were the **Holy Land shrine at Kalwaria Zebrzydowska** and the **Benedictine monastery at Tyniec.**

KALWARIA ZEBRZYDOWSKA—A VAST Christian park of
wooded paths and architecturally distinctive chapels that re-
create the biblical experience of Jesus, Mary, and the first disciples along two extensive trails known as the "Path of Our
Lord" and the "Path of Our Lady"—is located in the rolling
hills between Kraków and **Wadowice**. Karol Wojtyła knew
it well from his youth. A favorite pilgrimage destination,
Kalwaria Zebrzydowska also sponsored a dramatic three-
day passion play during Holy Week, to which the elder Karol
Wojtyła took his son shortly after Emilia Wojtyła died. The
Kalwaria passion play attracted thousands of pilgrims. Unlike its counterpart at Oberammergau in Germany (which is
held every decade), the annual passion play at Kalwaria was
not performed onstage; rather, it unfolded along some of the
trails of the shrine, the audience literally following the action

Beginning of the Path of Our Lord, Kalwaria Zebrzydowska

from station to station along the traditional *Via Crucis,* as in Jerusalem. Thus the audience at the Kalwaria passion play "lived" the last days of Christ's earthly life "with" the Lord, his mother, the holy women, the disciples, the people of Jerusalem, and the Romans. The Poles who came to Kalwaria did so not to watch a tale from the Bible but to live *inside* the biblical story.

This idea—living inside or through the biblical story—is as old as the New Testament. For St. Paul, according to the biblical scholar N. T. Wright, "the way to be saved is not by believing that one is saved. The way to be saved is by believing in Jesus as the crucified and risen Lord." That belief is life-transforming—or ought to be. If the Resurrection truly changed everything in history and the cosmos—if the saving power of God was revealed in the Jewish Messiah, who by his death and resurrection was constituted the New Adam in whom the divine mercy of God was extended to all humanity—then the affirmation that "Jesus is Lord" cannot be compartmentalized in a cupboard of our lives marked "religion." To say "Jesus is Lord" is to see the world with new eyes—to see the world as the arena of salvation history, which is unfolding in and through what the world knows as world history. That new way of seeing creates a new way of living, which Christians have called for two millennia life "in the Spirit": the Holy Spirit, the third Person of the Trinity and the bond of love between the Father and the Son, whom the Son promised to send upon his brothers and sisters as the bond of charity among them.

The Christian way of seeing and living creates new forms of human solidarity and community, in which there is "neither

Jew nor Greek, there is neither slave nor free, there is neither male nor female, for you are all one in Christ Jesus" (Galatians 3:28). And those new communities live in a distinctive way: they care for the sick, not only their own but others' as well; they do not expose unwanted children but cherish the gift of life as a gift of God; they treat honestly with their neighbors; they are faithful to their spouses; they live (as the second-century *Letter to Diognetus* summed up these distinctive qualities) as if every country were a homeland, even though their true homeland lies elsewhere. For they have a new Master, who told worldly power in the hour of his extremity that "my kingship is not of this world" (John 18:36), and it is his Kingdom that draws their deepest loyalty.

This is the entire thrust of St. Paul's letters to the new Christian communities: you must learn what it means to have a new Master, through whom you learn to see things afresh; you must learn to "see" and to think within the biblical story; you must reimagine your lives, putting aside the old ways (either the old ways of conceiving the Jewish Messiah or the old pagan ways) in order to think of your lives as playing within the great drama of salvation history. As N. T. Wright sums it up, because "the ultimate 'exodus' had now occurred in and through Jesus," Paul's new Christians must allow themselves "to be transformed by a biblically based renewal of the mind," in what amounted to a subversion-by-inversion of worldly ways of seeing and thinking. And this, in the final analysis, is what it means to enter the Kingdom of God, here and now, by being "born of water and the Spirit" (John 3:5).

That this new way of seeing, thinking, and living is no easy business is also made clear by Paul's letters: whether it's the backsliding Galatians or the prideful Corinthians or the fretting Thessalonians, no one, it seems, gets it right all the time, or perhaps even most of the time. Putting on the biblical way of seeing the world, living the meaning of the confession that "Jesus is Lord," is a lifelong process. That is why Cardinal Karol Wojtyła could often be found walking the pathways of Jesus and Mary at Kalwaria Zebrzydowska. In those hours of prayer and reflection, during which he pondered both the mysteries of salvation history and the decisions he had to make as the chief shepherd of the Church of Kraków, he was renewing his commitment to live his life as a priest and bishop inside the biblical story.

Some might think this spiritual romanticism. It was not. It was biblical realism of the highest order—the realism of the Kingdom breaking into history, here and now. To put on "the mind of Christ" (1 Corinthians 2:16) is to look at the world and the Church through Christ's eyes. That unique perspective helped Karol Wojtyła to resist the tyranny of the possible: the world's claims that some things just were the way they were (like the communist refusal to permit a church to be built in Nowa Huta and the postwar division of Europe) or the Church's resistance to change (based on the comforting idea that, well, we've always done it *this* way). Seeing the world and the Church through biblical lenses helped Karol Wojtyła see possibilities where others saw only obstacles; to see around and over the walls of the here and now, because the pathway to the future had already been defined by the new and definitive Exodus, Christ's Passover from death to life, in which the Kingdom of God had broken into history.

Almost two thousand years after St. Paul urged his Corinthians and Galatians and Thessalonians to see this way, Karol
Wojtyła could see this way (and could empower others to see
this way) because he believed in the truth of God's revelation
in the Bible. His daily immersion in Holy Scripture, which
continued until the last hours of his life, was far more than
a close study of some compelling ancient texts; it was an encounter with the living God, who in the inspired words of the
Bible revealed not just ideas about himself but himself. Thus
in his walks along the pathways of Kalwaria Zebrzydowska,
Wojtyła lived the truth to which he helped give expression at
the Second Vatican Council, in the Council's Dogmatic Constitution on Divine Revelation:

> It pleased God, in his goodness and wisdom, to reveal
> himself and to make known the mystery of his will
> [cf. Ephesians 1:9]. His will was that men should have
> access to the Father, through Christ, the Word made
> flesh, in the Holy Spirit, and thus become sharers in
> the divine life [cf. Ephesians 2:18; 2 Peter 1:4]. By this
> revelation, then, the invisible God [cf. Colossians 1:15;
> 1 Timothy 1:17], from the fullness of his love, addresses
> men as his friends [cf. Exodus 33:11; John 15:14–15] and
> moves among them [Baruch 3:38], in order to invite
> and receive them into his own company. This economy
> of revelation is realized by deeds and words, which are
> intrinsically bound up with each other. As a result,
> the works performed by God in the history of salva-
> tion show forth and bear out the doctrine and realities

Basilica of Sts. Peter and Paul and courtyard, Benedictine Abbey at Tyniec

signified by the words; the words, for their part, proclaim the works and bring to light the mystery they contain. The most intimate truth which this revelation gives us about God and the salvation of man shines forth in Christ, who is himself both the mediator and the sum total of revelation.

THE VENERABLE BENEDICTINE monastery at Tyniec was another place of spiritual retreat for Karol Wojtyła during his service as archbishop of Kraków. As a young man, he had been attracted to the contemplative life, trying twice to join the Carmelites: his first approach, during World War II, was rebuffed on the grounds that the community was accepting no novices during the turmoil of the occupation; then, when he spoke about the matter with Archbishop Sapieha during

his seminary years, the archbishop told him that he must fin-
ish what he had begun by entering the clandestine archdiocesan seminary.

Still, throughout his life, this man of genuine mystical
gifts, who found in contemplative prayer the spiritual energy
to lead his active life, sought ways to link contemplation to
action. On his first visit to Paris during his postwar studies in
Rome, he would tell a startled friend that the bustling Paris
Metro was "a superb place for contemplation." Hiking in the
mountains with his *Środowisko,* he would drift to the back
of the line after a day of walking and conversation, and his
friends would understand that this was his private time, his
time for silent conversation with the Lord who comes, not in
wind or earthquake or fire, but as a "still small voice" (1 Kings
19:12). So it was natural for him to come, time and again, to
Tyniec, where an ancient monastic community lived the life
of prayer and work prescribed in the *Rule of St. Benedict.* Here
were men dedicated to both contemplation and action, although in a different way than his own.

The consecrated religious life—life under permanent vows
of poverty, chastity, and obedience, typically lived in community under a distinctive rule of life—was for Karol Wojtyła
a kind of spiritual reactor core, an ecclesiastical furnace of
grace, that energized the entire Church. The life of the vows
might mean, in the case of the strictest contemplative communities, a withdrawal from the world and from regular
contact with the rest of the Church. But this withdrawal was
precisely for the sake of the world and the Church: a life of
prayer and intercession that could not be self-centered, but
which was radically God-centered and other-directed.

In his 1996 apostolic exhortation *Vita Consecrata* (The Consecrated Life), John Paul II approached the life of the vows—the kind of life from which he drew strength during his retreats at Tyniec—through a biblical lens. The consecrated life, he wrote, was a life of immersion in *philokalia,* "love of the divine beauty," and the principal biblical touchstone for it was the Transfiguration. There, on Mt. Tabor, Peter, James, and John were overwhelmed by the beauty of the transfigured face of Christ, the Anointed One of God to whom Moses and Elijah, the Law and the Prophets, bear witness. The Transfiguration is thus a privileged moment to experience the unity of God's revelation to the People of Israel and in his Son—which is the unity of the Bible. And the consecrated life is an extension of the experience of the Transfiguration into the ongoing life of the Church in history.

In *Vita Consecrata,* John Paul II drew on his experience of Tyniec and other such places of *philokalia* to remind a busy world of the truth that, while Martha's hospitality was an important service to her friend Jesus, Mary had chosen the "good portion" (Luke 10:42), the better way. The world of contemplation, John Paul taught, cannot be measured by any criteria other than its own. Men and women who give up everything to listen to the Lord, to intercede for others, and to serve in ministries of charity as an expression of their love of the Lord's beauty are, in the biblical way of seeing things, living the most radical form of discipleship: they have given up everything to follow the Master. They do not require the world's validation, least of all in terms of a criterion of "usefulness." Their witness, like the witness of Tyniec over the centuries, is its own validation.

At Tyniec, Karol Wojtyła also refined his understanding of how the consecrated life and its three vows are useful challenges to the wisdom of the late modern and postmodern worlds. The vow of obedience challenges a culture that imagines that "freedom" and "obedience" are antinomies at war with each other; life inside the Transfiguration story and the vow of obedience displays the truth that genuine freedom comes from living in obedience to the truths inscribed in the world and in us. The vow of poverty, John Paul wrote in *Vita Consecrata,* offers a similar challenge to worldly orthodoxies: in this case, a prophetic challenge to "the idolatry of anything created," which can manifest itself in such worldly bad habits as consumer frenzy and the degradation of environmental responsibility into Gaia worship. And then there is chastity, which postmodernity perhaps finds most puzzling. Chastity, John Paul taught, not only challenges modern hedonism, important as that is, but because we all fail to live the chaste lives we ought, persistence in the commitment to chastity is, even amidst sin, "a witness to the power of God's love manifested in the weakness of the human condition." For the consecrated person, who also faces challenges to chaste living in a sex-saturated culture, "attests that what many have believed impossible becomes, with the Lord's grace, possible and truly liberating."

PLACES SUCH AS Tyniec, where men have striven to follow the life of the vows for centuries, thus remind the whole Church to look with longing and awe on the beauty of the Lord, to keep our gaze fixed on his Holy Face, and, in doing so, to find

the "peace of Christ," which we wish one another in the celebration of the Eucharist. That peace, in turn, enables the disciples of Christ to live the evangelical vocation in which all were
baptized: the missionary vocation to display the beauty of the
Lord, so that others can come to know that the human thirst
for happiness, for beatitude, is only satisfied in an abandon-
ment of self to the embrace of God.

Kalwaria Zebrzydowska and Tyniec

Kalwaria Zebrzydowska
Route 52, between Kraków and Wadowice

When travel to the Holy Land was still a daunting prospect,
replica "Calvaries" became a popular form of devotion in six-
teenth- and seventeenth-century Europe. Kalwaria Zebrzy-

Fifth Station chapel (Simon of Cyrene), Kalwaria Zebrzydowska

Sixth Station (Veronica), Kalwaria Zebrzydowska

dowska (Zebrzydowski's Calvary) is one of the greatest expressions of the deep and intuitive connection that Christians throughout the centuries have felt with the places of salvation history, and of the Christian call to live inside the biblical story. Today, the Holy Land shrine in the hills near Wadowice, which hosts a million visitors annually, includes a Franciscan monastery, a great basilica, and more than forty distinctive chapels, located along four miles of trails, the intertwined "Path of Our Lord" and "Path of Our Lady." Listed in 1999 as a UNESCO World Heritage Site, the shrine, with its baroque landscaping and mannerist architecture, reflects in great detail the original plan created four hundred years ago.

The story of Kalwaria Zebrzydowska begins with a pious nobleman, Mikołaj Zebrzydowski, the regional governor of Kraków, whose property outside the city included the mountain of Żarek (really a high hill). There, in 1600, Zebrzydowski commissioned the building of the Church of the Holy Cross—according to one tradition, because of a vision his wife had experienced. The Church of the Holy Cross on Żarek was soon complemented by another chapel, built nearby and modeled on the Holy Sepulcher in Jerusalem. Zebrzydowski was struck by the similarity between the topography of his extensive holdings and that of the Holy Land—Żarek seemed to resemble Golgotha, while the hill of Lanckorona evoked the Mount of Olives. So he decided to build a whole series of chapels across the rolling landscape of his property, in memory of events from the passion, death, and resurrection of Christ. To help give the project authenticity, Zebrzydowski commissioned his friend Fr. Feliks Żebrowski—priest, astronomer, and mathematician—to help design the shrine, and Żebrowski developed a system of measurement to map the urban landscape of Jerusalem upon the Polish countryside.

By 1617, twenty-four chapels, which extended the traditional Way of the Cross while following its basic outline, had been built, some in a highly creative style (the chapel of the fourth station, for example, which commemorates Jesus's meeting his mother on the way to Calvary, is in the shape of a heart). After Zebrzydowski's death in 1620, his son, Jan, continued his father's work, adding a second group of chapels that commemorated scenes from the life of Mary. Today, forty-two chapels are located along the two trails of Jesus and Mary, which intersect at various points—most strikingly in the Chapel of the Assumption, suggesting with considerable theological insight, and long before the dogmatic definition of the Assumption in 1950 and the teaching of the Second Vatican Council, that Mary, first of disciples, is also the first fruit of the redemptive work of her Son. In addition to the annual passion play, Kalwaria Zebrzydowska has long hosted a great annual pilgrimage on the Solemnity of the Assumption, which draws pilgrims from all over southern Poland.

Jan's son, Michał Zebrzydowski, took up his grandfather's and father's work, enlarging the Franciscan monastery on the property and building a special chapel within the main church to house a miraculous icon of the Blessed Virgin Mary of Kalwaria (which, according to pious tradition, cried tears of blood in 1641).

Michał Zebrzydowski's daughter, Anna Zebrzydowska, inherited the property on her father's death in 1667. Anna married Jan Karol Czartoryski, which brought the property into the care of another noble family. When Anna died in 1668, Czartoryski married Magdalena Konopacka, who extended the nave of the basilica and added the two towers to its facade. Magdalena Czartoryska died in 1694, leaving the property to her son, Józef, who completed many of the projects his mother had begun.

Many of the European Calvaries were granted the same indulgence that pilgrims received (under the proper conditions) for making the Way of the Cross in the Holy Lands. Pope Paul V granted this privilege to pilgrims at Kalwaria Zebrzydowska in 1612.

The Basilica of the Madonna of the Angels

Kalwaria's principal church has grown from the chapel first built by Mikołaj Zebrzydowski on the model of the Holy Sepulcher in Jerusalem. Designed by the Italian Jesuit architect Giovanni Maria Bernardoni, it was finished by the Flemish architect and jeweler Paul Baudarth in 1609. Later dedicated to the Madonna of the Angels, it was consecrated by the bishop of Kraków on October 4, 1609, together with the adjacent Franciscan monastery.

In 1654–67, Michał Zebrzydowski enlarged the church and monastery, giving the latter the appearance of a baroque castle, while also adding the baroque side chapel to house the miraculous Madonna of Kalwaria. The church has remained the same ever since, although the monastery was enlarged again at the beginning of the nineteenth century. In 1910, plans to

Basilica of the Madonna of the Angels, Kalwaria Zebrzydowska

enlarge the basilica were denied authorization by local cultural authorities, to safeguard the original character of the historic church.

The Chapels

Many of the first chapels at Kalwaria Zebrzydowska were deigned by Paul Baudarth, who incorporated both mannerist influences from the Netherlands and traditional elements of Polish architecture, incorporating distinctive symbols, such as gates, roses, and hearts, into his plans. Based upon Baudarth's design, each chapel is distinguished by a unique design feature.

Among those built between 1605 and 1617 were (in order of construction) the chapels of Pilate's Praetorium, the Holy Sepulcher, the Mount of Olives, the Arrest of Jesus, the House of Annas, the House of Caiphas, Herod's Palace, the Sepulcher of the Mother of God, the House of the Mother of God, the Taking Up of the Cross, the Ascension, the Last Supper, the Heart of Mary, the Second Fall, St. Raphael, and the Hermitage of St. Mary Magdalene. Only four structures have been added since the seventeenth century: the chapels of the Third Fall of Christ in 1754, the Weeping Women of Jerusalem in 1782, St. John Nepomucene in 1824, and the Angels' Chapel in 1836.

The Benedictine Abbey at Tyniec

ul. Benedyktyńska, 37
Tyniec

The Benedictine Abbey at Tyniec, the oldest monastic foundation in Poland, is nestled amidst picturesque forests and perched on a rocky limestone escarpment above the Vistula

River between Kraków and Oświęcim, some seven miles from the Kraków Old Town.

The monastery was founded in 1044 by King Kazimierz the Restorer after a devastating Czech raid on Polish land in 1039 and a pagan uprising; Kazimierz believed that the Benedictines would help restore order in the region while helping reevangelize a country that threatened to fall back into pagan ways. (Historians speculate that the king's mother, Richeza of Lotharingia, influenced her son to invite Benedictines from her native city, Cologne, to Tyniec.) The Benedictines were housed at Wawel until the completion of the first Romanesque abbey church and monastery, around 1075. Kazimierz I's successors became "cofounders" of Tyniec by granting the monastery new properties, and over the centuries, the monastery's footprint grew to accommodate an expanding Benedictine community, with new wings being added to the abbey.

Despite its current atmosphere of peace and serenity, life at Tyniec has not always fulfilled the injunction in the *Rule of St. Benedict* that those living in the monastery were "not to be worried or experience distress." Located on the heavily traveled Vistula River, the monastery was sacked time and again by invaders on their way to bigger prizes in Kraków, thus demonstrating that the easy trade routes along the river, while a source of Poland's economic vitality, were also a factor in Poland's strategic vulnerability. The surrounding landscape offered no points of natural defense against aggressors, and, as in Kraków, fire was another common hazard.

The first significant attack upon the abbey came in 1259, during a Mongol invasion of Poland, as the invaders looted and destroyed much of the vulnerable monastery en route to

Memorial of the
Confederation of Bar and John
Paul II memorial, Benedictine
Abbey at Tyniec

Kraków. The buildings were quickly rebuilt—now with defensive fortifications.

The fourteenth century saw damage caused by both Tatar raids and Czech marauders. What was left of the original Romanesque abbey church was torn down in the fifteenth century and rebuilt in Gothic style.

The Swedish "Deluge" of 1655–60 witnessed the complete destruction of the monastery at Tyniec, after which the abbey was rebuilt in baroque style, with a new library added to the complex. Further eighteenth-century remodeling introduced rococo to the abbey church, and new fortifications (including a number of defensive gates linked through an angled corridor) were built, modeled on much-besieged Wawel.

In 1772, the monastery suffered massive damage during a civil war between Poles who wanted to reassert Polish independence and those more closely allied with Russian interests. The abbey complex was taken over and used as a fortress by the Polish patriots of the Confederation of Bar (so named for the Ukrainian town where the rebellion was declared). For months, the stone structures were pounded with artillery fire by the pro-Russian forces camped on the opposite bank of the Vistula River. Several buildings along the riverside were destroyed and never rebuilt.

The Partitions of Poland found the monastery and the neighboring town of Tyniec subsumed within the Austrian Empire as part of the province of Galicia. This, too, created enormous difficulties, as a decree of September 8, 1816, signed by the Habsburg emperor Francis I, dissolved the abbey. Like other Benedictine abbeys (including the monastery at Norcia, birthplace of St. Benedict), the property at Tyniec fell into disrepair as the monks were dispersed, although some valuables were salvaged by neighboring parishes and other monasteries. A fire in 1839 consumed the remaining wooden roofs of the crumbling monastery, and in 1844 the last monk of Tyniec died.

In the 1930s, with the support of monks from St. Andrew's Abbey in Bruges, Belgium, Benedictine life in Poland was reborn. On July 29, 1939, eleven Benedictine monks returned to Tyniec, just weeks before the outbreak of World War II and the depredations of the German occupation. Thus extensive refurbishing of the property did not start again until 1947. In 1968, the seat of the abbot was returned once again to the abbey church of Sts. Peter and Paul, but the political and economic circumstances of Poland's communist period stymied the full restoration of the historic abbey and its lands, which was only completed at the beginning of the twenty-first century with the help of the European Union.

The Abbey

The fifteenth-century Polish historian Jan Długosz once declared the abbey the "gem of the motherland." Unfortunately, numerous attacks and conflagrations have left the abbey strewn with "what used to be here." The monastic buildings all show signs of having been something else previously; archways have been filled in and doorways blocked off, with detailed lintels left behind. Yet despite the extensive rebuilding, the complex still reflects the *Rule of St. Benedict;* over the course of nine centuries, the monks have recast the property to accommodate their needs and customs.

The monastery is a large rectangle built around several courtyards. Approached from the Vistula, the two towers of the abbey church stand out against the skyline. Distinctive features within the abbey include a 131-foot-deep well, dug in the early tenth century; the wooden shelter protecting it from the elements is from the early seventeenth century. The monastic library, repeatedly demolished, is now decorated with rococo elements.

The monastery at Tyniec today also houses the Benedictine Institute of Culture, the Abbey Guest House, and the Lapidarium Museum, and offers retreats for visitors as well as cultural and educational events.

The Basilica of Sts. Peter and Paul

While little of the fabric of the late-Gothic, fifteenth-century structure remains, the abbey church, now a minor basilica, still retains a number of Gothic elements, including a Gothic presbytery or sanctuary. Several of the altars were created by the eighteenth-century Italian sculptor Francesco Placidi, who was also involved in renovations at the *Mariacki* in Kraków's **Main Square**. Placidi was noted for his use of black marble; his high altar in the abbey church features the Holy Trinity and the abbey patrons, the apostles Peter and Paul.

The Blessed Sacrament chapel is on the southern side of the presbytery and was previously the Marian chapel. The side altars flanking the presbytery honor St. Peter and St. Mary Magdalene.

The monastic choir, which occupies the entire eastern portion of the church, is notable for its early seventeenth-century choir stalls. Paintings along the southern wall above the stalls depict important events in the life of St. Benedict, including the temptation of Benedict; the miracle of Brother Placid being saved from drowning by Brother Maur; Benedict and his monks being fed by angels after giving away their food to the needy; and a victory over Muslims (either Turks or Tatars) attributed to the miraculous intervention of St. Benedict. The paintings above the stalls on the north side of the choir feature other Benedictine saints and Pope St. Gregory the Great, who in the late sixth century sent Benedictines to England (led by the man whom history would know as St. Augustine of Canterbury) to begin the evangelization of that land.

The nave of the basilica is baroque, as are its side chapels, dedicated to St. Benedict (co-patron of the abbey church); All Saints; St. Anne, the mother of Mary; and St. Scholastica, the sister of St. Benedict.

The late baroque pulpit by Franciszek Józef Mangoldt uses

extensive maritime imagery. The base of the pulpit is orna-
mented with a net and the heads of fish rising out of a wave. A
carved ship symbolizes the Church; the figure of Christ evokes
the image of the Lord at the helm of his Church amidst rough
storms—appropriately enough, given the monastery's dramatic
history. A woman, symbol of faith, walks on the surface of the
water next to the ship; in one hand she holds an anchor, the
symbol of hope, and in the other a dove, the symbol of love.
(Popular throughout Europe in baroque churches, ship-pulpits
can also be found in Kraków churches dedicated to St. Andrew
and to the Body of Christ [Corpus Christi].)

A new, simple, and modern side chapel, from 1981, is dedicated to the Holy Cross. The traditional stations on the interior
pillars are a recent addition to the abbey church, as is the new
organ.

Karol Wojtyła made a five-day retreat at Tyniec before his
ordination as a bishop in 1958. In 1975, Cardinal Wojtyła took
part in celebrations marking the abbey's nine hundredth anniversary. On August 19, 2002, during his final pilgrimage to
Poland, John Paul II spontaneously decided to visit the Abbey of
Tyniec, for what turned out to be the last time. [C.G.]

Papal Pathways

"Barka" mosaic, "Be Not Afraid" Center

Błonia Krakowskie

Living Stones, Confirmed in Faith

The Nine Days of John Paul II—his first papal pilgrimage to Poland from June 2 through June 10, 1979—were days on which the history of the world pivoted and the course of postwar history was bent in a more humane direction. Prior to the Nine Days, the division of Europe into two hostile camps seemed a permanent fixture of world politics. So did the captivity of the peoples of central and eastern Europe, whose states had been taken over by communists at the end of World War II and whose liberties had been abrogated by those who claimed to be on the "side of history." Prior to the Nine Days, a nuclear arms race that threatened the future of humanity seemed likely to grind on indefinitely. Viewed from the perspective of June 1, 1979, the Berlin Wall seemed an ugly, fixed marker in world affairs. Nine days later, something had changed in the texture of world politics, and in a fundamental way. Ten and a half years after that, the Berlin Wall was gone.

That John Paul II played a pivotal role in the collapse of European communism is now widely accepted by scholars of the Cold War. As Yale's John Lewis Gaddis put it, "When John

"You Are 'Rock'" memorial, Błonia Krakowskie

Paul II kissed the ground at the Warsaw airport on June 2, 1979, he began the process by which communism in Poland— and ultimately everywhere—would come to an end." But the nature of the revolution John Paul ignited is not so well understood, nor is the character of the Nine Days. Viewed as the world thinks of history, the Nine Days of John Paul II seem like a great act of national catharsis, a psychological earthquake that inspired virtually an entire nation to resistance against its oppressors. And certainly something like that happened, between June 2 and June 10, 1979, from the Baltic to the Tatras, from Wrocław to Przemyśl, and at every point in between. Viewed from the surface of world history, the Nine Days of June 1979 were Poland's longed-for recompense for the sufferings of the past forty years, and from that new national energy new forms of political action evolved.

True enough. But in wrestling with the question of what happened in Poland between June 2 and June 10, 1979, it is important to go deeper. One needs to look *inside* history, to see those days through biblical lenses and to read the Nine Days from inside the unfolding story of salvation history, in order to get to the truth of what John Paul II accomplished—or, as he would have insisted, what the Holy Spirit accomplished through him, in the Nine Days.

For rarely if ever in the modern world has the Catholic claim that salvation history *is* world history, read in its proper depth and against its most ample horizon, been so vindicated as it was from June 2 through June 10, 1979, and in the months and years that followed.

DURING THE NINE Days, John Paul II never spoke once of politics, economics, or what we normally think of as public affairs. Aside from the necessary courtesies at the beginning and end of his journey and at the key stops along the way, the Polish pope acted as if the Polish government simply did not exist. In dozens of homilies, addresses, and lectures, and in his spontaneous remarks, the words "communism" and "Marxism-Leninism" never crossed his lips. Rather than re-butting communist falsifications of philosophy and the Polish communist rewriting of Polish history head-on, John Paul II ignored them, as if they were a bad dream, a nightmare from which his people were awakening. Instead of a straightfor-ward critique of communism's false ideas of the human per-son, human community, human origins, and human destiny, John Paul II offered a bold, uncompromising, compelling, and compassionate catechism lesson, reminding his people of the truths the Catholic Church proclaimed: the truths that had helped give Poland its distinctive character, the truths that had seen it through hard times in the past, the truths that thoroughly refuted the lies on which communism rested—the truths along which the path toward a better future might be found.

Or to put it a little differently, throughout the Nine Days John Paul II preached and taught a great lesson in national dignity and led a historic reclamation of national identity— and did so by references to Poland's "baptism" in 966 and its "confirmation" in the martyrdom of St. Stanisław. Time and again, whether talking with students or professors, Polish highlanders or Polish workers, the Polish pope came back to the same great theme, saying, in effect, "You are not who *they* say you are. Permit me to remind you who you *really* are. Reclaim that identity—own the truth of it—and you will find tools of resistance *they* cannot match."

The result was a revolution of conscience, in which the kindling that had been gathering for decades was ignited by a forthright call to Christian conversion, expressed in uniquely Polish terms. Out of that revolution of conscience came, thirteen months later, the shipyard strikes in Gdańsk that gave birth to the Solidarity movement. And over a long, hard decade, filled with sacrifice and sanctified by the blood of martyrs such as Blessed Jerzy Popiełuszko, Solidarity triumphed, the Wall came tumbling down, and history took a course no one could have imagined on June 1, 1979.

THE TEXTS OF John Paul II's Nine Days are replete with wonderful imagery, at once both Christian and Polish, that had an electrifying effect on his audiences. And those audiences were, in truth, congregations, for the entire Nine Days was like a vast national retreat, in which eleven million Poles participated in person, and the rest of the country participated by radio and television (the reliable radio source being the American-funded Radio Free Europe). On June 2 in Warsaw, on the Vigil of Pentecost, John Paul stood at an outdoor altar in Victory Square and cried out to the Holy Spirit, "Renew the face of the earth—of *this* land!" At Gniezno on June 3, he asked whether it was not obvious that it was Christ's will that "this Polish pope, this Slav pope, should at this precise moment manifest the unity of Christian Europe," itself the result of the "rich architecture of the Holy Spirit." Then he answered his own question: "Yes. It is Christ's will, it is what the Holy Spirit disposes. . . . We shall not return to the past! We shall go toward the future! 'Receive the Holy Spirit!' [John 20:22]. Amen!" At the Jasna Góra monastery in Częstochowa, home of the Black Madonna, he spoke movingly of listening here to "the beating heart of the Church and of the motherland in the heart of the Mother," where one heard "the echo of the life of the whole nation in the heart of its Mother and Queen."

And then he came back to his "beloved Kraków."

Those were days of overflowing emotion and deep reflection—and great banter. When the crowds of young people began to clamor for him one night outside **Franciszkańska 3,** in the midst of a spontaneous songfest, John Paul climbed onto a windowsill and began teasing his young followers: "It's bad enough being the pope in Rome. It would be far worse being the pope in Kraków, spending all the time standing at this window with no time to sleep and no time to think." At midnight, he sent them off with a laugh: "You are asking for a word or two, so here they are—Good night!"

The climax of the Nine Days came on the Kraków Commons, the **Błonia Krakowskie,** on June 10, at the closing Mass of the pilgrimage. Before more than a million Poles, John Paul, who had begun his re-catechesis of the nation in Warsaw on June 2 with the theme of Baptism, brought his epic voyage to a conclusion by a reflection on Confirmation: the confirmation of a nation, in the martyrdom of St. Stanisław, and the confirmation he prayed for his people as he left, a new confirmation in the power of the Holy Spirit:

> When I . . . began with you to prepare for the ninth centenary of the death of Saint Stanisław . . . we all were still under the influence of the one thousandth anniversary of the Baptism of Poland which was celebrated in . . . 1966. Under the influence of this event and remembering the figure of Saint Adalbert . . . whose life was connected in our history with the epoch of our Baptism, the figure of Saint Stanisław seems to point . . . to another sacrament, which is part of the Christian's initiation into the faith and into the life of the Church. This is the sacrament . . . of the anointing or Confirmation. . . .
>
> Just as a baptized person comes to Christian maturity by means of this sacrament of Confirmation, so Divine Providence gave to our nation, after its Baptism, the historical moment of Confirmation. Saint Stanisław, who was separated by almost a whole century from the period of the Baptism and from the mission of Saint

Adalbert, especially symbolizes this moment by the fact that he rendered witness to Christ by his own blood. In the life of each Christian, usually a young Christian because it is in youth that one receives this sacrament— and Poland too was then a young nation, a young country—the sacrament of Confirmation must make him or her become a "witness to Christ" according to the measure of one's own life and proper vocation. . . .

This is the sacrament which brings to birth within us a sharp sense of responsibility for the Church, for the Gospel, for the cause of Christ in the souls of human beings, and for the salvation of the world.

The sacrament of Confirmation is received by us only once in our lifetime (just as Baptism is received only once). All of life which opens up in view of this sacrament assumes the aspect of a great and fundamental test: a test of faith and of character. St. Stanisław has become, in the spiritual history of the Polish people, the patron of this great and fundamental test of faith and of character. In this sense we honor him also as the patron of the Christian moral order. In the final analysis the moral order is built up by means of human beings. This order consists of a large number of tests, each one a test of faith and of character. From every victorious test the moral order is built up. From every failed test moral disorder grows.

We know very well from our entire history that we must not permit, absolutely and at whatever cost, this disorder. For this we have already paid a bitter price many times.

This is therefore our meditation on the seven years of St. Stanisław, on his pastoral ministry in the See of Kraków ... [and] all of this leads us today to a great and ardent prayer for the victory of the moral order in this difficult epoch of our history.

Then, having inserted the thousand-year history of Poland into the rhythm of salvation history by reference to Baptism and Confirmation, John Paul spoke to his people of a new outpouring of the Holy Spirit in a new laying on of hands, as at Confirmation, in which Christians are strengthened in the three theological virtues of faith, hope, and love:

Today, then, as I stand here in these broad meadows of Kraków and turn my gaze towards Wawel and Skałka ... I wish to fulfill again what is done in the sacrament of Confirmation, the sacrament that he symbolizes in our history. I wish what has been conceived and born of the Holy Spirit to be confirmed anew through the Cross and Resurrection of our Lord Jesus Christ, in which our fellow-countryman St. Stanisław shared in a special way.

Allow me, therefore, like the bishop at Confirmation, to repeat today the apostolic gesture of the laying on of hands. For it expresses the acceptation and transmission of the Holy Spirit, whom the Apostles received from Christ himself after his Resurrection, when, "the doors being shut" (John 20:19), he came and said to them: "Receive the Holy Spirit" (John 20:22).

This Spirit, the Spirit of salvation, of redemption, of

conversion and holiness, the Spirit of truth, of love and of fortitude, the Spirit inherited from the Apostles as a living power, was time after time transmitted by the hands of the bishops to entire generations in the land of Poland. This Spirit, whom the bishop who came from Szczepanów transmitted to the people of his time, I today wish to transmit to you, as I embrace with all my heart yet with deep humility the great "Confirmation of history" that you are living.

I repeat therefore the words of Christ himself: "Receive the Holy Spirit" (John 20:22).

I repeat the words of the Apostle: "Do not quench the Spirit" (1 Thessalonians 5:19).

I repeat the words of the Apostle: "Do not grieve the Holy Spirit" (Ephesians 4:30).

You must be strong, dear brothers and sisters. You must be strong with the strength that comes from faith. You must be strong with the strength of faith. You must be faithful. Today, more than in any other age, you need this strength. You must be strong with the strength of hope, hope that brings the perfect joy of life and does not allow us to grieve the Holy Spirit.

You must be strong with love, which is stronger than death. You must be strong with the love that: "is patient and kind; . . . is not jealous or boastful; . . . is not arrogant or rude . . . does not insist on its own way; . . . is not irritable or resentful; . . . does not rejoice at wrong, but rejoices in the right . . . bears all things, believes all things, hopes all things, endures all things. Love never ends (1 Corinthians 13:4–8).

You must be strong with the strength of faith, hope and charity, a charity that is aware, mature and responsible and helps us to set up the great dialogue with man and the world rooted in the dialogue with God himself, with the Father through the Son in the Holy Spirit, the dialogue of salvation.

And finally, he begged his people to remain true to the gift they had been given:

And so, before I leave you, I wish to give one more look at Kraków, this Kraków in which every stone and every brick is dear to me. And I look once more on my Poland.

So, before going away, I beg you once again to accept the whole of the spiritual legacy that goes by the name of "Poland," with the faith, hope and charity that Christ poured into us at our holy Baptism.

I beg you

—never lose your trust, do not be defeated, do not be discouraged;

—do not on your own cut yourselves off from the roots from which we had our origins.

I beg you

—have trust, and notwithstanding all your weakness, always seek spiritual power from him from whom countless generations of our fathers and mother have found it;

—never detach yourselves from him;

—never lose your spiritual freedom, with which "he makes a human being free";

—Never disdain charity, which is "the greatest of these" and which shows itself through the Cross. Without it human life has no roots and no meaning.

All this I beg of you

—recalling the powerful intercession of the Mother of God at Jasna Góra and at all her other shrines in Polish territory;

—in memory of Saint Adalbert who underwent death for Christ near the Baltic Sea;

—in memory of Saint Stanisław who fell beneath the royal sword at Skałka.

All this I beg of you.

Amen.

IN THE SIXTEENTH chapter of Matthew's gospel, in response to Jesus's question about who people say he is, Simon makes the confession of faith, "You are the Christ, the Son of the living God" (Mathew 16:16). The Lord Jesus responds by changing Simon's name to Peter, meaning "rock," and promises him that "on this rock I will build my Church, and the powers of death shall not prevail against it" (Matthew 16:18). As the Catholic Church understands the papacy, the Bishop of Rome, the successor of St. Peter, is, like Peter, the "rock" on which the Church is built. John Paul II was that rock-like figure on the Błonia Krakowskie on June 10, 1979: a self-evident truth to Poles, commemorated in a memorial stone at the place where John Paul preached that day. But he was not a solitary rock. Rather, like Peter, John Paul II called others to ongoing conversion: he called his people to be the living stones of 1 Peter

2:5—the living stones from which a new future of freedom and responsibility and solidarity could be built.

They responded, and history changed for the better.

The Kraków Commons

Błonia Krakowskie

Bounded by al. Marszałka Ferdynanda Focha, al. 3 Maja, and ul. Piastowska

The *Błonia Krakowskie* (Kraków Meadows, or Kraków Commons) is a curiosity in a modern European city: its 120 acres make it the largest undeveloped open space in a European city center. The Błonia is also the only natural meadow within a European city's limits never to have been touched by a permanent structure; plans drawn up in the past—housing for German officials or an emergency airport during World War II—never materialized.

The Błonia's history is controverted due to a lack of clear records, but it seems that the land was initially donated in the twelfth century to Norbertine nuns by a noble leaving on pilgrimage to the Holy Land. After two centuries, the sisters exchanged this unspoiled parcel of land with the civil authorities, trading it for a manor house near the city center in 1366. While one history claims that the agreement led to a four-hundred-year-long dispute between the nuns and the city after the manor house burned down, it is clear that the meadow was used extensively as pastureland by peasants to graze their cattle.

For centuries, Kraków suffered from epidemics; as medical knowledge grew, the spring flooding and swampy conditions of the Błonia and other nearby areas were considered a significant threat to public health. Early in the nineteenth century, measures were taken to drain the wetlands. One unanticipated result was that the meadow could now play host to large gatherings. In 1809, swelling crowds came for a military parade of Napoleon's troops, organized by Prince Józef Poniatowski, the governor of the newly established Duchy of Warsaw. The Błonia was later used for city celebrations, such as the five hundredth anniversary of the Battle at Grunwald, and for balloon and air shows.

While generally used today as a park for recreation, concerts, and exhibits, the Błonia has another distinctive feature. In 1965, a hotel was being built nearby, and the developers were concerned by what they regarded as unsightly cattle still grazing in the meadow. The city council sought to remove the undesirable bovines, but discovered a decree dating back to Queen Jadwiga in the fourteenth century, establishing the Błonia as a cow pasture. Soviet-style bureaucracy made changes to the antique decree impossible, so the Błonia today is one of the only legal cow pastures within a European city's limits.

The site is located between Kraków and the old village of Zwierzyniec, which has been subsumed into the city. The meadow serves as a green link between residential neighborhoods and the city center, and is now flanked by two new soccer stadiums. The Błonia is also close to two commemorative mounds honoring the great Polish leaders Tadeusz Kościuszko and Józef Pilsudski.

Protected as a National Heritage Site since 2000, Kraków's meadow is best known for the Masses celebrated there by Pope John Paul II in 1979, 1983, 1987, 1997, and 2002. His visits have been commemorated on a twenty-six-ton granite rock quarried from the Morskie Oko lake in the Tatra Mountains, engraved with the biblical citation "You are 'rock'" (Matthew 16:18).

On April 8, 2005, hundreds of thousands who had not made the trip to Rome for the funeral of Poland's greatest son gathered here to watch John Paul II's funeral Mass on large-screen televisions.

In May 2006, Pope Benedict XVI celebrated Mass on the Błonia during his papal pilgrimage to Poland. [C.G.]

Łagiewniki

Trust in Divine Mercy

On August 17, 2002, on his last pilgrimage to his Polish homeland, Pope John Paul II consecrated the **Basilica of Divine Mercy** in the Łagiewniki district of Kraków. In doing so, he completed a journey that had begun six decades before, when the young Karol Wojtyła walked past the convent where Sister Maria Faustina Kowalska had died after several years of receiving visions of the Merciful Jesus, who passed on to her the message of Divine Mercy. In those hard times, when the weight of an inhuman totalitarianism bore heavily on the young worker and clandestine seminarian, Karol Wojtyła found strength in prayer in the red-brick convent chapel where Sister Faustina, who had died the year before World War II overwhelmed Poland, would later be interred.

That journey from Łagiewniki in the war years to Łagiewniki in the first years of the twenty-first century had also passed through Auschwitz-Birkenau, on John Paul II's first pastoral pilgrimage to Poland. There the Pope, in his homily, remembered just what had happened to humanity, such that Sister Faustina's visions were of the greatest consequence for the future:

Chapel of the Convent of the Sisters of Our Lady of Mercy

Can it still be a surprise to anyone that the pope born and brought up in this land, the pope who came to the see of Saint Peter from the diocese in whose territory is situated the camp of Oświęcim, should have begun his first encyclical with the words *Redemptor Hominis* [The Redeemer of Man] and should have dedicated it as a whole to the cause of man, to the dignity of man to the threats to him, and finally to his inalienable rights that can so easily be trampled on and annihilated by his fellow men? . . .

I am here today as a pilgrim. It is well known that I have been here many times. So many times! And many times I have gone down to Maximilian Kolbe's death cell and stopped in front of the execution wall and passed among the ruins of the cremation furnaces of Brzezinka. It was impossible for me not to come here as pope. . . . I have come to pray with all of you who have come here today and with the whole of Poland and the whole of Europe. Christ wishes that I who have become the Successor of Peter should give witness before the world to what constitutes the greatness and the misery of contemporary man, to what is his defeat and his victory.

I have come and I kneel on this Golgotha of the modern world, on these tombs, largely nameless like the great tomb of the Unknown Soldier. I kneel before all the inscriptions that come one after another bearing the memory of the victims of Oświęcim in languages: Polish, English, Bulgarian, Romany, Czech, Danish, French, Greek, Hebrew, Yiddish, Spanish, Flemish, Serbo-Croat, German, Norwegian, Russian, Romanian, Hungarian, and Italian. In particular I pause . . . before the inscription in Hebrew. This inscription awakens the memory of the People whose sons and daughters were intended for total extermination. This People draws its origin from Abraham, our father in faith (cf. Romans 4:12), as was expressed by Paul of Tarsus. The very people that received from God the commandment "Thou shalt not kill," itself experienced in a special measure what is meant by killing. It is not permissible for anyone to pass by this inscription with indifference.

Finally, the last inscription: that in Polish. Six million Poles lost their lives during the Second World War: a fifth of the nation. Yet another stage in the centuries-old fight of this nation, my nation, for its fundamental rights among the peoples of Europe. Yet another loud cry for the right to a place of its own on the map of Europe. Yet another painful reckoning with the conscience of mankind.

The human conscience had been seared by the horrors of the mid-twentieth century; some might say that that conscience had been permanently scarred, to the point where it had become insensible to further slaughters of innocents, whether those be innocents who were elderly and considered "useless" and "disposable," innocents who were of a different ethnic or tribal stock (as in the Balkans and Rwanda in the 1990s), innocents who had not yet been born. John Paul II knew the sorrows of late modern humanity as well as anyone; he knew them in microcosm (from the prayer requests that flooded the papal apartment and which he prayed through each day), and he knew them in macrocosm (from his own experiences of the war and of totalitarian repression, as well as from the reports he received daily from his representatives around the world). Yet, knowing all that, John Paul II refused to concede that humanity's twentieth-century scars condemned the world to a future as horrific as the recent past. Indeed, he held precisely the opposite view. To the end, he was a witness to hope, as he described himself at the United Nations in 1995. And that hope gave rise to a great vision of human possibility:

We must not be afraid of the future. We must not be afraid of man. It is no accident that we are here. Each and every human person has been created in the "image and likeness" of the One who is the origin of all that is. We have within us the capacities for wisdom and virtue. With these gifts, and with the help of God's grace, we can build in the next century and the next millennium a civilization worthy of the human person, a true culture of freedom. We can and we must do so! And in doing so, we shall see that the tears of this century have prepared the ground for a springtime of the human spirit.

It is important to underscore that this was not optimism. Optimism is a matter of optics, of how we look at things, and that can change simply by looking at things differently. John Paul II's message was one of hope, and, moreover, a hope based on faith: faith in the capacity of the Divine Mercy to cleanse the seared conscience of humanity, such that it could call the men and women of the twenty-first century from fear and disdain to compassion and solidarity.

POPE FRANCIS CITED God's mercy time and again in his first years in the Chair of Peter, quickly establishing a theme for his pontificate. Some found this new, but the truth of the matter is that it was John Paul II who put Divine Mercy at the center of the Catholic Church's proclamation to the twenty-first-century world: by canonizing Sister Faustina as the first saint of the Great Jubilee of 2000 and the new millennium and by lifting up the message of Divine Mercy as the remedy for the scarred consciences and the guilt that humanity carried from the charnel house that was the twentieth century.

That confidence in the mercy of God was not meant to soften or blunt John Paul II's call to moral responsibility. The merciful Father is always ready to forgive, but his prodigal sons and daughters must first acknowledge their failures, an acknowledgment that opens the heart and soul to receive the Father's gift of restored dignity. The moral law, John Paul taught throughout his pontificate, is not an arbitrary set of rules designed by a coercive God to inhibit human freedom. Rather, the moral law offered on Mt. Sinai (as the Pope put it there in February 2000) was "written on the human heart" before it was written on tablets of stone. And those tablets, in turn, were a Magna Carta of liberation, rules for righteous living that were intended to prevent the People of Israel from falling back into the bad habits of slaves. The Ten Commandments, John Paul taught at Sinai, are "the law of freedom: not the freedom to follow our blind passions, but the freedom to love, to choose what is good in every situation." And in that choosing, John Paul concluded, humanity grasps the truth about itself: "In revealing himself on the Mountain and giving his law, God revealed man to himself. Sinai stands at the very heart of the truth about man and his destiny."

Still, we all fail, and fail frequently. That is one of the reasons the Lord Jesus promised his disciples the gift of the Holy Spirit. As John Paul put it at the consecration of the Divine Mercy Basilica, "It is the Holy Spirit, the Comforter and the Spirit of Truth, who guides us along the ways of Divine Mercy. By convincing the world 'concerning sin and righteousness and judgment' (John 16:8), he also makes known the fullness of salvation in Christ. . . . On the one hand, the Holy Spirit enables us, through Christ's Cross, to acknowledge sin, every sin, in the full dimension of evil which it contains and inwardly conceals. On the other hand, the Holy Spirit permits us, again through Christ's Cross, to see sin in the light of the *mysterium pietatis,* that is, of the merciful and forgiving love of God . . . [so that] this 'convincing concerning sin' also becomes a conviction that sin can be laid aside and that man can be restored to his dignity as a son beloved of God."

BY SOLEMNLY ENTRUSTING the world to Divine Mercy at Łagiewniki in August 2002, John Paul II was, once again, repeating the call to fearlessness with which he opened his pontificate: "Be not afraid!" And in repeating that call in this place, he linked it to a prayer of St. Faustina recorded in her diary, *Divine Mercy in My Soul*—a prayer that speaks to the

Room in which St. Maria Faustina Kowalska died

struggles every Christian soul experiences, from the temptations of the world and the weaknesses of human nature, from failures and guilt, as we seek to remain affixed to the Cross of Christ:

> My Jesus, you see that your holy will is everything to me. It makes no difference to me what you do to me. You command me to set to work—and I begin calmly, although I know that I am incapable of it; through your representatives, you order me to wait—so I wait patiently; you fill my soul with enthusiasm—but you do not make it possible for me to act; you attract me to yourself in heaven—and you leave me in this world; you pour into my soul a great yearning for yourself— and you hide yourself from me. I am dying of the desire to be united with you forever, and you do not let death come near me. O will of God, you are the nourishment and delight of my soul. When I submit to the holy will of God, a deep peace floods my soul.
>
> O my Jesus, you do not give a reward for the successful performance of a work, but for the good will and labor undertaken. Therefore, I am completely at peace, even if all my undertakings and efforts should be thwarted or should come to naught. If I do all that is in my power, the rest is not my business. And therefore the greatest storms do not disturb the depths of my peace; the will of God dwells in my conscience. [*Diary*, 952]

"Jesus, I trust in you." That confession of confident faith, simple yet so hard for self-consciously modern twenty-first-century men and women to make, was, John Paul II was convinced, the message the world most needed to hear in order to cope with the burden of grief and guilt that had crossed from the twentieth century to the twenty-first. That message can be embraced conceptually. But perhaps it is best embraced in prayer—prayer like the Litany of Divine Mercy found in the diary of St. Faustina:

+ GOD'S LOVE IS THE FLOWER—MERCY THE FRUIT.
Divine Mercy, gushing from the bosom of the Father, I
trust in you.
Divine Mercy, greatest attribute of God, I trust in you.
Divine Mercy, incomprehensible mystery, I trust in you.
Divine Mercy, fount gushing forth from the mystery of
the Most Blessed Trinity, I trust in you.
Divine Mercy, unfathomed by any intellect, human or
angelic, I trust in you.
Divine Mercy, from which wells forth all life and
happiness, I trust in you.
Divine Mercy, better than the heavens, I trust in you.
Divine Mercy, source of miracles and wonders, I trust in
you.
Divine Mercy, encompassing the whole universe, I trust
in you.
Divine Mercy, descending to earth in the Person of the
Incarnate Word, I trust in you.
Divine Mercy, which flowed from the open wound in the
Heart of Jesus, I trust in you.
Divine Mercy, enclosed in the Heart of Jesus for us, and
especially for sinners, I trust in you.

*Divine Mercy, unfathomed in the institution of the
Sacred Host, I trust in you.*

*Divine Mercy, in the founding of Holy Church, I trust in
you.*

*Divine Mercy, in the Sacrament of Holy Baptism, I trust
in you.*

*Divine Mercy, in our justification through Jesus Christ, I
trust in you.*

*Divine Mercy, accompanying us through our whole life, I
trust in you.*

*Divine Mercy, embracing us especially at the hour of
death, I trust in you.*

*Divine Mercy, endowing us with immortal life, I trust in
you.*

*Divine Mercy, accompanying us in every moment of our
lives, I trust in you.*

*Divine Mercy, shielding us from the fire of hell, I trust in
you.*

*Divine Mercy, in the conversion of hardened sinners, I
trust in you.*

*Divine Mercy, astonishment for Angels,
incomprehensible to Saints, I trust in you.*

*Divine Mercy, unfathomed in all the mysteries of God, I
trust in you.*

*Divine Mercy, lifting us out of every misery, I trust in
you.*

*Divine Mercy, source of our happiness and joy, I trust in
you.*

*Divine Mercy, in calling us forth from nothingness to
existence, I trust in you.*

Divine Mercy, embracing all the works of his hands, I
    trust in you.
Divine Mercy, crown of all God's handiwork, I trust in
    you.
Divine Mercy, in which we are all immersed, I trust in
    you.
Divine Mercy, sweet relief for anguished hearts, I trust
    in you.
Divine Mercy, only hope of anguished souls, I trust in
    you.
Divine Mercy, repose of hearts, peace amidst fear, I trust
    in you.
Divine Mercy, delight and ecstasy of holy souls, I trust in
    you.
Divine Mercy, inspiring hope against all hope, I trust in
    you. [Diary, 949]

Łagiewniki

The Łagiewniki district of Kraków and the adjacent Borek
Fałęcki district (home to the **Solvay chemical factory,** where
Karol Wojtyła worked during World War II) are south of the
Kraków Old Town and east of Dębniki. Many new commercial
developments have reshaped the district since the communist
crack-up in 1989; so have developments in Kraków's religious
life, including the building of the **Divine Mercy Basilica** near
the Shrine of Divine Mercy in the **Convent of the Sisters of Our
Lady of Mercy** and the new **"Be Not Afraid" Center** in memory of St. John Paul II. The Kraków city administration has taken

note of Karol Wojtyła's long relationship with Łagiewniki–Borek Fałęcki by naming new boulevards in the area after John Paul's favorite contemporary Polish poet, Zbigniew Herbert, and two of the Pope's old friends: Jerzy Turowicz, longtime editor of *Tygodnik Powszechny,* and Father Józef Tischner, philosopher and chaplain of the First Solidarity Congress in 1981.

The Convent of the Sisters of Our Lady of Mercy
ul. Siostry Faustyny (Kraków-Łagiewniki tram stop)

The striking red-brick neo-Gothic convent was built in the late nineteenth century thanks to a benefaction by Count Aleksander Lubomirski, who asked Cardinal Albin Dunajewski, the archbishop of Kraków, to use funds Lubomirski had donated to

Convent of the Sisters of Our Lady of Mercy

aid girls and women "in moral need." In 1889, Cardinal Dunajewski, knowing of the Congregation of the Sisters of Our Lady
of Mercy and their work with women and girls, passed the donation to the sisters to build a convent and mercy house for their
apostolate. The sisters created a model home, in which the principle of respect for the dignity of the human person was linked
to confidence in the mercy of God, and moral renewal was complemented by training in skills that would enable the girls and
women who came to the home to eventually reenter society.

The communist authorities seized the convent's home for
troubled women and a considerable part of the adjacent property in 1962, leaving only one wing of the convent building,
the chapel, and a small garden. Undaunted, the sisters then
organized a center for socially troubled youngsters inside the
convent, which they ran until 1991; the former properties were
returned to the sisters in 1989. Today, the sisters host a board-
ing school as well as a high school, a hairdressing school, and
a culinary school for troubled girls ages fifteen to eighteen in
need of vocational training.

The convent has also housed a novitiate for the Sisters of
Our Lady of Mercy since 1893; the two-year program prepares
novices for religious life and the community's apostolic work,
which now includes pastoral care for the two million pilgrims
who annually visit the Shrine of Divine Mercy.

Sister Maria Faustina Kowalska, who received the Message
of Divine Mercy in her visions of Jesus and the Devotion to the
Divine Mercy that has reshaped Catholic piety throughout the
world, lived in the convent at Łagiewniki from 1926 until 1928,
and then from 1936 until her death on October 5, 1938. Born
in Głogowiec in 1905, Faustina joined the Sisters of Our Lady

of Mercy in Warsaw in 1925 and later lived in convents in Płock and Wilno (Vilnius). In Płock, on February 22, 1931, she had her first vision of the Merciful Jesus, clothed in a white garment with two rays emanating from his heart, who instructed her to have his image painted with the signature "Jesus, I trust in you"—a task Sister Faustina was able to complete in Wilno with the assistance of her confessor, Father Michał Sopocko (himself now beatified). In September 1935, while still in Wilno, Sister Faustina received a vision of the Divine Mercy Chaplet, which has become one of the most popular forms of Catholic devotional life throughout the world.

Sister Faustina was transferred to Kraków in 1936, suffering from what was thought to be tuberculosis. She died two years later, on October 5, 1938, in the convent of the Sisters of Our Lady of Mercy, and was buried on October 7. Her relics were later transferred to the convent's chapel of St. Joseph (today's Shrine of Divine Mercy), where they rest on the side altar to the left of the sanctuary, under the miraculous image of the Divine Mercy (by Adolf Hyła).

Archbishop Karol Wojtyła, having cleared up Roman misunderstandings about the apostle of Divine Mercy and her diaries, opened the diocesan process for the beatification and canonization of Sister Faustina in 1965. Sister Faustina was beatified on April 18, 1993, and canonized on April 30, 2000, at a ceremony in which John Paul II announced that the Church would thereafter celebrate the Octave (or Second Sunday) of Easter as Divine Mercy Sunday. In his homily at the canonization Mass, John Paul said of the new saint that "the message she brought is the appropriate and incisive answer that God wanted to offer to the questions and expectations of human beings in our time, marked by terrible tragedies." The liturgical memorial of St. Maria Faustina Kowalska is celebrated on October 5.

The Divine Mercy Sanctuary

The Convent Chapel, the Shrine of Divine Mercy, is the heart of the Divine Mercy complex at Łagiewniki. Here, St. Faustina prayed. Here, she received many of her visions. Here she professed her religious vows, and here her mortal remains rest. Here, too, is the famous image painted by Adolf Hyła during World War II, renowned for the favors received by many who prayed before it. Here, young Karol Wojtytła often paused for prayer on his way to and from the Solvay chemical works during World War II. Here, young Father Wojtyła would come

Basilica of Divine Mercy

to celebrate Mass, as he would come to pray as bishop and pope.

The Basilica of Divine Mercy was consecrated by John Paul II on August 17, 2002, during which the Pope solemnly entrusted the entire world to the Divine Mercy. The basilica, designed by Kraków architect Witold Cęckiewicz, is a large ellipsoidal structure, intended to evoke images of a ship, the 253-foot-tall observation tower suggesting a mast. The main sanctuary's stark interior focuses the pilgrim's attention on the Divine Mercy image and the golden, globe-shaped tabernacle beneath. The ground floor of the basilica houses a chapel dedicated to St. Faustina and several side chapels, one of which includes striking contemporary mosaics of the martyrs of central and eastern Europe.

At the end of the consecration ceremony in 2002, John Paul II spontaneously reminisced about his first experience of the Łagiewniki site:

> At the end of this solemn liturgy, I desire to say that many of my personal memories are tied to this place. During the Nazi occupation, when I was working in the Solvay factory near here, I used to come here. Even now I recall the street that goes from [the neighborhood of] Borek Fałęcki to Dębniki that I took every day going to work on the different turns with the wooden shoes on my feet. They're the shoes that we used to wear then. How was it possible to imagine that one day the man with the wooden shoes would consecrate the Basilica of the Divine Mercy at Łagiewniki of Kraków?

Pope Benedict XVI continued the papal tradition of honoring the Divine Mercy Shrine by visiting it during his pilgrimage to Poland in 2006. While there, the Bavarian pope unveiled a new statue of John Paul II on the deck of the observation tower.

The Divine Mercy complex also includes a conference and retreat center and pilgrim housing.

"Be Not Afraid" Center

Near the Divine Mercy Sanctuary is the new "Be Not Afraid" Center dedicated to the legacy of Pope John Paul II. The complex overlooks the Borek Fałęcki district, where the young Karol Wojtyła worked in the Solvay chemical factory during the Second World War.

The Center was first founded in 1995 as the John Paul II Institute by Cardinal Franciszek Macharski. In 1997, during a papal

"Be Not Afraid" Center

visit to the city, Pope John Paul visited and blessed the Institute's new location at Kanonicza 18 in Kraków's Old Town.

In 2006, the archbishop of Kraków, Cardinal Stanisław Dziwisz, established the Center as a corporate ecclesiastical public body under the Archdiocese of Kraków. The founding decree states that the Center intends "to commemorate the great legacy and pontificate of . . . Pope John Paul II, so that his example and word are passed on to future generations."

The center's name, "Be Not Afraid," refers to the public inauguration of John Paul II's pontificate on October 22, 1978, when the centerpiece of the papal homily was the clarion call, "Be not afraid! Open the doors to Christ!"

The Center's main chapel features contemporary mosaics by the Jesuit Marko Ivan Rupnik, and includes a panel given by the men and women of Karol Wojtyła's *Środowisko:* Jesus and the disciples in a boat on the Sea of Galilee, recalling Karol Wojtyła's last kayaking trip with his friends in 1978, during which they frequently sang the hymn "Barka." The altar on

Main chapel, "Be Not Afraid" Center

the ground floor chapel houses a relic of John Paul II's blood. The rest of the ground floor is devoted to various chapels: one, given by the miners at Wieliczka, is decorated with salt sculptures and statues; another contains the original marble stone slab beneath which John Paul II was first buried in the grottos of St. Peter's Basilica; a funerary chapel created by John Paul II houses the remains of two Polish cardinals, Andrzej Deskur and Stanisław Nagy. [C.G.]

St. Kinga: salt statue carved by Wieliczka miners, "Be Not Afraid" Center

In Thanksgiving

Lessons in the Tatras

When John Paul II died on April 2, 2005, the world experienced a swirl of emotions in which the predominant motif seemed to be thanksgiving: thanks that this man who had touched so many lives was now where he had always wanted to be, in the Father's house; thanks for all that he had done for the Church and for the cause of freedom; thanks—indeed, awestruck gratitude—that such a life was possible in these times and circumstances.

That sense of thanksgiving was entirely appropriate, but it also spoke to the nature of the man for whom and to whom so many were grateful. For over the course of almost eighty-five years, Karol Wojtyła had become a living embodiment of thanksgiving, because he had become a thoroughly eucharistic disciple of Jesus Christ. "Eucharist" comes from the Greek εὐχαριστία (thanksgiving). And as daily celebration of the Holy Eucharist was at the center of Karol Wojtyła's day for seven and a half decades, the grace of the sacrament transformed his life, over time, into a continual act of thanksgiving, rendering grateful worship to God for the gifts of creation, redemption, and sanctification—the gifts bestowed by Father,

Stained glass window depicting the assassination attempt of May 13, 1981, Sanctuary of Our Lady of Fatima, Zakopane

Son, and Holy Spirit. That he died shortly after his longtime secretary, Stanisław Dziwisz, had celebrated the Mass for Divine Mercy Sunday at his bedside underscored in a striking way just how Karol Wojtyła, Pope John Paul II, had lived.

THE PEOPLE OF Poland gave thanks for John Paul II throughout his pontificate and have continued to do so since his death. Poland is replete with squares, streets, and institutions named for Poland's noblest son; statues of John Paul can be found in innumerable public spaces throughout Poland; his travels throughout the country are remembered by many roadside markers and shrines. Of all these acts of thanksgiving and remembrance, one that captures the life and spirit of Karol Wojtyła in a singularly powerful way may be found in **Zakopane,** the principal town in the Polish Tatras. There, the highlanders of Poland built by hand a wooden *votum* church, dedicated to Our Lady of Fatima, in thanksgiving for the life of John Paul II being spared on May 13, 1981, when Mehmet Ali Agca shot the Pope in his front yard, St. Peter's Square.

During his third Polish pilgrimage in 1987, John Paul II described himself as a "man of the mountains." Born in the foothills of the Beskidy range, he had climbed the mountains of Leskowiec and Babia Góra with his father when he was a boy. Later, as priest and bishop, he had frequently gone into the mountains to hike and ski—and to pray and reflect. He knew the names of virtually every peak in the Tatras, but above all he knew the Polish highlanders and admired their robust faith and Polish patriotism. For all that he was a world-class intellectual, John Paul II had a deep respect for untutored popular piety; in his ministry as priest and bishop, he sought to refine that piety, but he never demeaned or deprecated it. And in the case of the *Górale,* the Polish mountain people, popular piety had fed a fierce determination to live as their traditions taught they should live, no matter what Nazis or communists had to say about the matter.

Karol Wojtyła's was an essentially gentle soul, but there was also something of the toughness of the *Górale* about him. Until his body betrayed him in the last decade of his life—and even amidst that decade's struggles—he was a physically tough man, capable of withstanding both deprivation and pain, an athlete and outdoorsman who kept himself fit for whatever tasks lay ahead. He was both tenderhearted and tough-minded: his convictions, which he had arrived at through careful thought and prayer, in obedience to God and the Church, could not be shaken, either by totalitarian threats or by media mockery. Above all, there was a spiritual tough-ness about John Paul II—the toughness of the genuine mystic, who feels the world's pain (and the Evil One's presence) more acutely than others; who absorbs those slings and arrows, and who bends but never breaks.

These qualities commended Karol Wojtyła to the *Górale,* even as he took from them some of their mountaineers' har-diness. And when they paid tribute to him by erecting the wooden *votum* church in Zakopane, the **Sanctuary of Our Lady of Fatima,** they did so in a way that demonstrated that, while the people of the Tatras may not have been trained theo-logians, they understood John Paul II from the inside. Thus while the casual tourist's eye will be immediately drawn to the two stained glass windows that depict the shooting of John Paul II in St. Peter's Square on May 13, 1981, and his pilgrim-age to Fatima on May 13, 1982 (during which he placed one of the bullets taken from his body in the crown of the statue of Our Lady of Fatima), a closer inspection of the *votum* church will draw the eye and heart and soul to two of the hand-carved stations of the cross: the fifth station, where it is John Paul II, with Simon of Cyrene, who helps carry the cross of Christ, and the twelfth station, where it is John Paul II, in place of the apostle John, who stands with the holy women beneath the cross of the dying savior.

The inscription over the entrance to the *votum* church de-scribes it as "a gift in gratitude for the rescue of the Holy Fa-ther on the 13th of May, 1981." The fifth and twelfth stations locate that day, as John Paul II located his life, within the ambit of salvation history, inside the story to which both Scripture and Tradition bear witness. That is why the *votum* church of

*Fifth Station, Sanctuary
of Our Lady of Fatima,
Zakopane*

Zakopane is so appropriate a gesture of thanksgiving for the life and ministry of the son of the mountains whom the world knew as Pope John Paul II.

CONTRARY TO A popular misunderstanding, neither the Catholic Church nor the pope "makes saints." The Catholic Church, through the pope, recognizes the saints that God has made. In 1983, John Paul II changed the process by which the Church recognizes those in whose lives God has acted with special effect with the apostolic constitution, *Divinus Perfectionis Magister* (The Divine Teacher of Perfection). Previously, in a process dating from the seventeenth century,

*Twelfth Station, Sanctuary
of Our Lady of Fatima,
Zakopane*

"saint-making" was something akin to a trial, in which the
candidate was posthumously subjected to an adversarial legal
proceeding, aimed at refuting claims to his or her sanctity;
candidacies that successfully ran that gauntlet, and for which
confirming miracles were then approved, were beatified and
canonized. John Paul changed the process to something that
resembled a doctoral seminar in history rather than a criminal trial. Now, in the process of gathering testimony for the
Positio, the critical biography of the candidate that is the centerpiece of the new process, witnesses are asked to reflect on
the life of the candidate through the prism of the theological
virtues (faith, hope, and love) and the cardinal virtues (prudence, justice, courage, and moderation) and to consider how
the candidate lived these virtues *heroically*—for that is the
classic measure of sanctity.

*Fatima shrine, Sanctuary
of Our Lady of Fatima,
Zakopane*

The theological virtues, as the Catholic Church understands them, are gifts of God that enliven our natural
capacities—"the pledge of the action of the Holy Spirit" in our
lives, as the catechism of the Catholic Church puts it. How
did Karol Wojtyła, Pope John Paul II, live those theological
virtues heroically?

Perhaps the best testimony to John Paul's heroic life of faith
came from one of his closest collaborators, Joseph Ratzinger,
who eventually succeeded him as Bishop of Rome. In a 1996
interview, Cardinal Ratzinger described John Paul's life of
faith in detail:

His personal meditation, his personal dialogue with God, is decisive for his life. He is a man of God, and his philosophy and theology are essentially born in his dialogue with God. The deepest source of what he says is that, every day, he is, for an hour, alone with his Lord and speaking . . . with him about all the problems of the world. But he is also seeking the face of God, and this is very important. In his meditations he is in personal contact with the Lord and thus directed to sanctity and sanctification. Before the literary sources, before the experiences of life, this dialogue with God is the central element in his spiritual and intellectual life.

But it's clear that the dialogue with God is also living from the dialogue with man. All his intellectual reflections helped him to be more intensive in his dialogue with God and in his pastoral experience, because dialogue is not an isolated and individual phenomenon, it is always with the Lord, for others: for the sanctification not only of his own person but to do the work of sanctification with the Lord in the world.

This "dialogue with God" was not without its dark nights; those were to be expected in someone as formed by Carmelite spirituality as John Paul II. But those dark nights were, for all their pain, experiences of purification, because Karol Wojtyła conformed his suffering—physical and spiritual—to the Cross of Christ.

At the United Nations in 1995, John Paul II explained why he was a man of hope and why his hope was not mere optimism. His hope, he said to the assembled powers of the world, was "centered on Jesus Christ," whose "Death and Resurrection ... fully revealed God's love and his care for all creation." Christian hope was always Christ-centered: its source was the "radiant humanity of Christ," the experience of which fills the Christian with hope for every human being. That hope also animated John Paul's conviction that sanctity is everywhere, and that God is profligate in his gifts of grace: one just had to learn to look for those gifts at work. John Paul II lived inside the biblical story and the story of salvation history, and because of this he was convinced that the Holy Spirit had not exhausted his gifts in the Upper Room at Pentecost.

John Paul II's heroic exercise of the virtue of hope helps explain two other facets of his personality. His intense interest in the person who was right in front of him was rooted not in mere curiosity but in the hope-filled conviction that here was someone in whom the grace of God was at work—someone for whom the Son of God had been incarnate, suffered, and died; someone called, like him, to sanctity. John Paul's hope also helps explain his lack of concern with closure (even as it illuminates his ability to see possibilities where others only saw obstacles and roadblocks): he did not demand immediate results from history, for his Easter faith—the source of his hope—taught him that God's purposes would ultimately be vindicated. Thus he was content to sow the seed, leaving it to others to gather in the harvest.

As for the "more excellent way" (1 Corinthians 12:31), John Paul II's capacity to live out the theological virtue of love was manifest early in his life; as his old seminary spiritual director (and later his auxiliary bishop in Kraków), Stanisław

Smoleński, once put it, young Karol Wojtyła "loved easily." That love was the source of his astounding energy, his ability to keep pouring himself out "like a libation" (2 Timothy 4:6) long beyond what the world might have thought "reasonable." And while Dorothy Day rightly wrote that Christian love is a "harsh and dreadful" thing because of the great demands of self-giving that it lays upon the radically converted disciple, it is also, finally, the source of joy, as it was for John Paul II: a happy man, even a cheerful man, despite all the burdens he bore.

Wojtyła's exercise of Christian love was, in the final analysis, deeply paternal, a way of self-giving he had learned first from his father, and later from Cardinal Sapieha. He lived his priesthood as a special form of spiritual paternity, calling others to maturity with that uniquely paternal combination of strength and compassion. And because he understood the universality of the human drama, his exercise of the virtue of love and his unique gift for spiritual paternity were deployed across the widest possible longitude—thus his remarkable ability to connect with people in an extraordinarily wide range of human and cultural circumstances.

This high-octane mixture of faith, hope, and love led, in Karol Wojtyła, to an exceptionally rich and compelling human personality. That he deployed that personality not to play the demagogue but to summon others to live compassionately and nobly in exercises of solidarity of which they might not have thought themselves capable, also says something about the role of humility in his life: a humility born of his priestly conviction that his vocational task was not to say, "Look at me," but to say, "Look at Jesus Christ."

———————

THE CENTRAL IDEA in Karol Wojtyła's philosophical ethics was what he called, in a 1974 lecture, the "Law of the Gift"— the countercultural claim that the more we give ourselves away, the more we come into possession of ourselves and become who we really are. But that's a bit abstract. Father Robert Barron suggests that we can grasp what John Paul II meant by the Law of the Gift by pondering the Gospel story of the multiplication of loaves and fishes, and the relationship of that story to the Holy Eucharist:

> Here is the spiritual "physics" behind the John Paul idea. Since God has no need of anything, whatever is given to him returns to the giver elevated and multiplied. Anything returned to God breaks, as it were, against the rock of the divine self-sufficiency and comes back, super-abundantly, to the giver. So in the Gospel story, the disciples have very little—two fish and five loaves—but they return these simple gifts to the Giver of all things, and they find them multiplied unto the feeding of the five thousand. The same principle holds in regards to the Eucharist. We bring a few tiny gifts to the Lord: bread, wine, and water. But they return to us infinitely enhanced as the Body and Blood of Jesus, and they serve to feed the deepest hunger of our hearts.

Karol Wojtyła, Pope St. John Paul II, not only identified the Law of the Gift philosophically; he lived it spiritually and pastorally, thus making himself into a grace-filled gift for others. That, ultimately, is the gift for which the mountaineers of the Polish Tatras were giving thanks in building the *votum* church in Zakopane. And that is the great lesson taught in these mountains, with John Paul II as a guide: living our lives as a gift for others, as our lives were a gift to each of us, is the pathway to beatitude, nourished by grace.

Zakopane

Zakopane is the largest town in the Tatra Mountains region of Poland and for decades was the summer home of many of Kraków's leading intellectuals and artists. Today, Zakopane is a major recreational center and a year-round destination for both tourists and Poles.

Sanctuary of Our Lady of Fatima
ul. Krzeptówki, 14

Wooden churches are a long-standing tradition in the Polish Tatras; nine of them were listed as UNESCO Heritage Sites in 2003. Constructed entirely of native timbers in a medieval design exclusive to the region, these churches, the gifts of noble families, were built by local highlanders, adapting wood to Gothic architectural elements usually created in stone. In keeping with this tradition of "national" or folk architecture, the people of the Tatras built a new church at Krzeptówki in Zakopane, as a thanksgiving gift for the "rescue" of John Paul II from the assassination attempt of May 13, 1981.

In his homily during the church's consecration in 1997, John

*Sanctuary of Our Lady
of Fatima*

Paul II spoke of the interweave of native piety and native architecture in the Polish mountains:

> Looking at your church, so beautifully decorated, I have
> before my eyes those wooden churches . . . which used
> to rise throughout Poland, but above all in Podhale and
> Podkarpacie: authentic treasures of popular architecture.
> All of them, like your own, were built with the cooperation
> of the pastors and faithful of the individual parishes. They
> were built by a common effort, so that the Holy Sacrifice
> could be celebrated there, so that Christ in the Eucharist
> would be together with his people day and night,
> at times of great joy and elation, and at times of trial,
> suffering and humiliation, and even on plain grey days.

The Church is a place of memory and yet of hope: it faithfully preserves the past while constantly pointing people toward the future, not only the future of time but also that of the afterlife. In churches we profess our belief in the forgiveness of sins, in the resurrection of the body, and in life eternal. Here we experience daily the mystery of the communion of saints. . . . I rejoice that in Zakopane and Podhale new churches have risen, magnificent monuments to the living faith of the people of this area. Their beauty matches the beauty of the Tatra Mountains and is the reflection of the same beauty spoken of in the inscription on the Cross by Wincenty Pol in Kościeliska Valley: "Nothing is greater than God."

The *votum* church was built in conjunction with a preexisting Shrine of Our Lady of Fatima, first established by the Pallottine fathers in 1946 as an apostolic center for spreading the message of Fatima. In 1961, Cardinal Stefan Wyszyński, primate of Poland and archbishop of Gniezno and Warsaw, gave the Pallottines a statue of Our Lady of Fatima originally donated by the bishop of Fatima. It was housed in a chapel next to the order's residence at Krzeptówki and traveled with the Pallottines around Polish parishes for twenty-seven years—a striking pilgrimage during the communist period. John Paul II crowned the statue when it was in Rome on October 21, 1987, his life having been providentially intertwined with the story of Our Lady of Fatima when, on her feast day, he was shot in St. Peter's Square—and, as he put it, "one hand fired, and another guided, the bullet."

The *votum* church was designed by Zakopane native

Stanisław Tylka. Its large front courtyard offers a panoramic view of Mt. Giewont and a towering statue of St. John Paul II with open hands of welcome. A large cross with John Paul II's papal coat of arms replicates the cross on top of Mt. Giewont, now over a century old: a cross of which John Paul also spoke in another homily in the Tatras: "Today I thanked God for the fact that your ancestors raised the cross on Giewont. That cross looks out over the whole of Poland, from the Tatras to the Baltic. And it says to the whole of Poland: *Sursum Corda*—lift up your hearts!"

The interior of the church was decorated by local artisans, who crafted the intricately hand-carved wooden pews, confessionals, choir loft, and baldachino. [C.G.]

Appendices

Polish Pronunciation

Pronunciation in Polish is more regular than in English. Once one learns the sound-value of the letters used in Polish, pronunciation is not that difficult.

The following rules and examples should be helpful.

The letters *ą* and *ę* are pronounced as a nasal *aw* and *en* in English.

C is pronounced as *ts* in English.

Ch is pronounced as a hard *h*, as in the Scottish "loch."

Cz is pronounced as *ch* in "church."

Dz is pronounced as *j* in "jeans."

I is pronounced as *ee* in "sweet."

J at the beginning of a word is pronounced as *y* in "yesterday."

J within a word is pronounced as long *i* as in "island."

Ł and *ł* are pronounced as *w* in "wood."

Ó and *ó* are pronounced as *oo* in "cool."

Ś and *ś* are pronounced as *s* in "sure."

Sz is pronounced as *sh* in "shutter."

W at the beginning of or within a word is pronounced as *v* in "victory."

W at the end of a word is pronounced as *f* as in "roof."

Y is pronounced as *y* in "myth."

Ż is pronounced as *zh* in "Zhivago."

The accent in Polish is almost always on the second-to-last syllable.

Thus, by way of examples:

Częstochowa is pronounced *chens-toe-HOE-vah.*

Dębniki is pronounced *denb-NEE-kee.*

Dziwisz is pronounced *JEE-vish.*

Jadwiga is pronounced *yahd-VEE-gah.*

Jerzy is pronounced *YARE-zhee.*

Kazimierz is pronounced *kah-ZHEE-meerzh.*

Mariacki is pronounced *mah-ree-AHTS-kee.*

Matejko is pronounced *mah-TAY-koh.*

Kraków is pronounced *KRAH-koof.*

Łagiewniki is pronounced *wah-ghee-ev-NEE-kee.*

Nowa Huta is pronounced *NOE-vah HOO-tah.*

Płaszów is pronounced *PWAH-shoof.*

Rakowicki is pronounced *rah-koe-VEETS-kee.*

Różana is pronounced *roo-ZHA-nah.*

Rynek Główny is pronounced *RIH-nek GWOOV-nee.*

Skałka is pronounced *SKOW-kah.*

Stanisław is pronounced *stan-EES-wahv.*

Środowisko is pronounced *shroe-doe-VEES-koe.*

Tyniecka is pronounced *tin-YETS-kah.*

Wadowice is pronounced *vah-doe-VEET-sah.*

Wawel is pronounced *VAH-vel.*

Wojtyła is pronounced *voy-TEE-wah.*

Zakopane is pronounced *zah-koe-PAH-nay.*

Examples of accents falling before the penultimate syllable include the following:

Błonia Krakowskie is pronounced *BWOE-nee-ah krah-KOFF-skee.*

Jagiellonian is pronounced *yah-ghee-eh-LOW-nee-en.*

Kalwaria Zebrzydowska is pronounced *kal-VAHR-ee-ah zeb-zhi-DOV-ska.*

Tyniec is pronounced *TIN-ee-ets.*

Władysław Jagiełło is pronounced *VWAH-dees-wahf yah-ghee-AY-woh.*

Polish Names in English

Aleksander = Alexander

Andrzej = Andrew

Aniela = Angela

Augustyn = Augustine

Emilia = Emily

Eugeniusz = Eugene

Feliks = Felix

Ferdynand = Ferdinand

Franciszek = Francis

Henryk = Henry

Ignacy = Ignatius

Jacek = James

Jadwiga = Hedwig

Jan = John

Jerzy (diminutive, Jurek) = George

Józef = Joseph

Juliusz = Julius

Kazimierz =Casimir

Karol (diminutive, Lolek) = Charles

Krystyna = Christina

Krzysztof (diminutive, Krysiu) = Christopher

Marcin = Martin

Michał = Michael

Mikołaj = Nicholas

Paweł = Paul

Rafał = Raphael

Stanisław = Stanislaus

Stefan = Stephen

Szczepan = Stephen

Szymon = Simon
Tadeusz = Thaddeus
Tomasz = Thomas
Wincenty = Vincent
Władyłsaw = Ladislaus
Wojciech = Adalbert
Zygmunt = Sigismund

Bolesław, Bronisław, Czesław, Danuta, Halina, Mieczysław, Mieszko, and Zbigniew are old Slavic or Polish names with no precise English equivalents.

Witold is derived from the Lithuanian Vytautas and has no English equivalent.

302

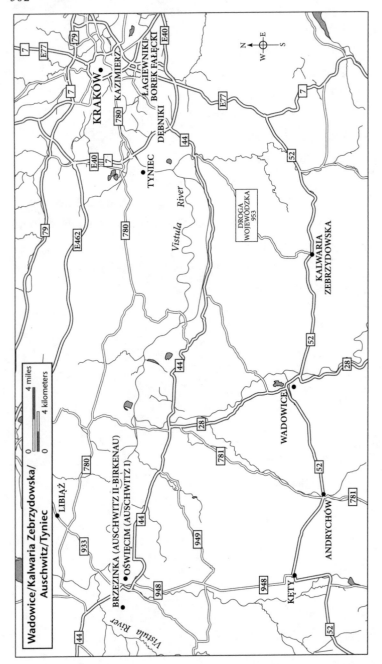

Wadowice/Kalwaria Zebrzydowska/
Auschwitz/Tyniec

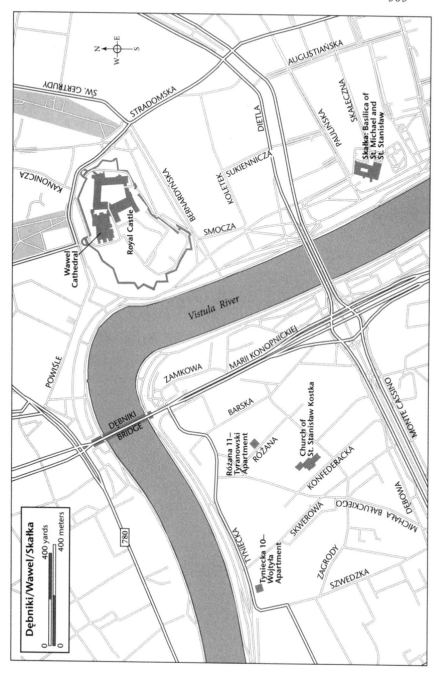

Dębniki/Wawel/Skałka

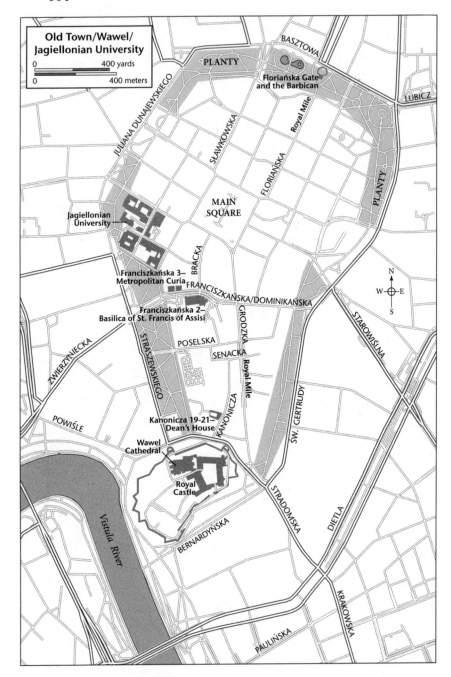

**Old Town/Wawel/
Jagiellonian University**

0 400 yards
0 400 meters

PLANTY

BASZTOWA

Floriańska Gate
and the Barbican

LUBICZ

JULIANA DUNAJEWSKIEGO

SŁAWKOWSKA

Royal Mile

FLORIAŃSKA

PLANTY

MAIN
SQUARE

Jagiellonian
University

BRACKA

Franciszkańska 3–
Metropolitan Curia

FRANCISZKAŃSKA/DOMINIKAŃSKA

Franciszkańska 2–
Basilica of St. Francis of Assisi

STRASZEWSKIEGO

POSELSKA

GRODZKA

Royal Mile

SENACKA

STAROWIŚLNA

N
W   E
S

ZWIERZYNIECKA

POWIŚLE

Kanonicza 19-21–
Dean's House

KANONICZA

ŚW. GERTRUDY

Wawel
Cathedral

Royal
Castle

STRADOMSKA

DIETLA

Vistula River

BERNARDYŃSKA

KRAKOWSKA

PAULIŃSKA

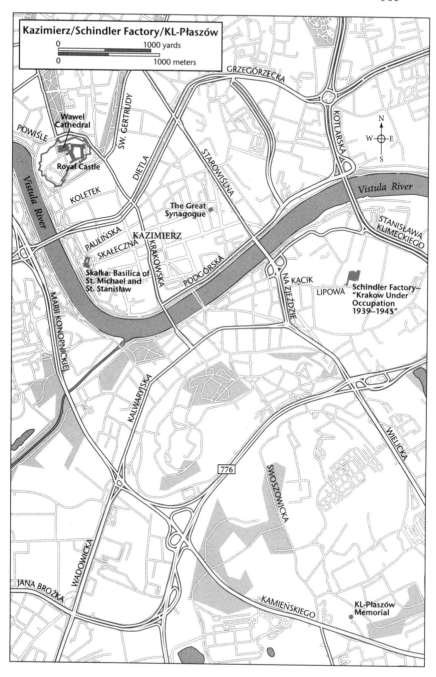

Kazimierz/Schindler Factory/KL-Płaszów

0   1000 yards

0   1000 meters

GRZEGÓRZECKA

KOTLARSKA

Wawel Cathedral

Royal Castle

SW. GERTRUDY

DIETLA

POWIŚLE

Vistula River

KOLETEK

STAROWIŚLNA

Vistula River

N
W—⊕—E
S

STANISŁAWA KLIMECKIEGO

The Great Synagogue

KAZIMIERZ

PAULIŃSKA

SKAŁECZNA

KRAKOWSKA

Skałka: Basilica of
St. Michael and
St. Stanisław

PODGÓRSKA

NA ZJEŹDZIE

KĄCIK

LIPOWA

Schindler Factory—
"Krakow Under
Occupation
1939–1945"

MARII KONOPNICKIEJ

KALWARYJSKA

WIELICKA

776

SWOSZOWICKA

WADOWICKA

JANA BROŻKA

KAMIEŃSKIEGO

KL-Płaszów
Memorial

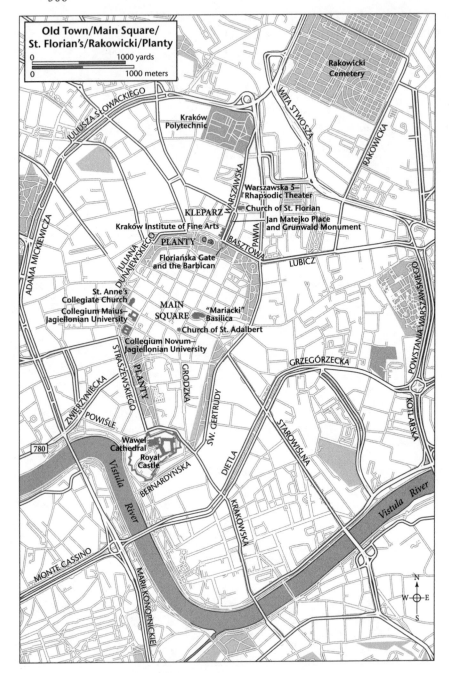

Old Town/Main Square/ St. Florian's/Rakowicki/Planty

0   1000 yards

0   1000 meters

Rakowicki Cemetery

JULIUSZA SŁOWACKIEGO

Kraków Polytechnic

WITA STWOSZA

RAKOWICKA

WARSZAWSKA

Warszawska 5– Rhapsodic Theater

Church of St. Florian

KLEPARZ

Jan Matejko Place and Grunwald Monument

Kraków Institute of Fine Arts

PAWIA

ADAMA MICKIEWICZA

JULIANA DUNAJEWSKIEGO

PLANTY

BASZTOWA

LUBICZ

Floriańska Gate and the Barbican

St. Anne's Collegiate Church

Collegium Maius– Jagiellonian University

MAIN SQUARE

"Mariacki" Basilica

Church of St. Adalbert

Collegium Novum– Jagiellonian University

POWSTANIA WARSZAWSKIEGO

GRZEGÓRZECKA

KOLARSKA

PLANTY

STRASZEWSKIEGO

GRODZKA

ŚW. GERTRUDY

STAROWIŚLNA

ZWIERZYNIECKA

POWIŚLE

780

Wawel Cathedral

Royal Castle

BERNARDYŃSKA

Vistula River

DIETLA

KRAKOWSKA

Vistula River

MONTE CASSINO

MARII KONOPNICKIEJ

N W E S

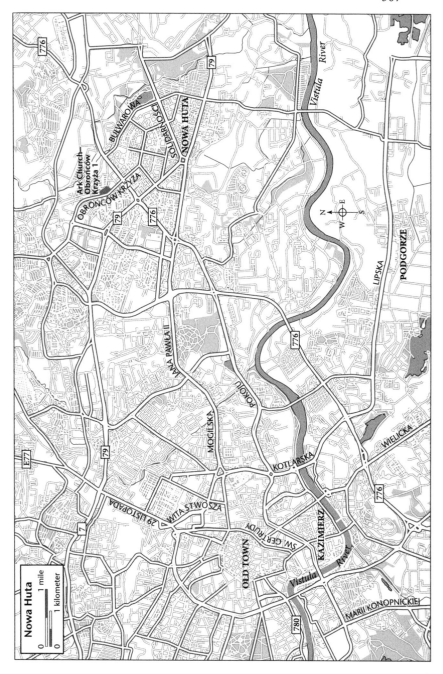

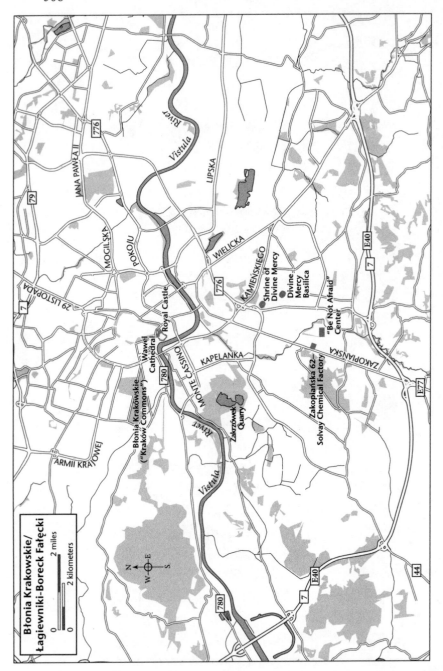

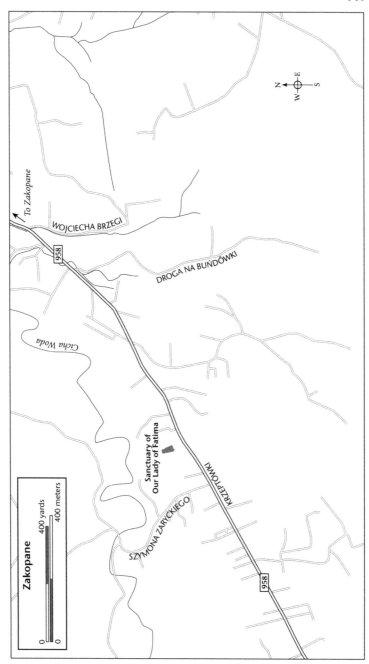

Zakopane

0 400 yards

0 400 meters

To Zakopane

WOJCIECHA BRZEGI

958

DROGA NA BUŃDÓWKI

Cicha Woda

Sanctuary of
Our Lady of Fatima

SZYMONA ZARYCKIEGO

KRZEPTÓWKI

958

N
W — E
S

Acknowledgments

This introduction to Kraków through the life of St. John Paul II has grown out of my experience of that wonderful city over more than twenty years.

I first came to Kraków in June 1991, while doing research for *The Final Revolution: The Resistance Church and the Collapse of Communism*. The city was much duller and far more gray in those days, but beneath the grime of communism I got a sense of the vibrancy waiting to be reborn. In 1994, I began coming to Kraków every July to teach in the Tertio Millennio Seminar on the Free Society, a unique project in international Catholic education that was encouraged by John Paul II and which I've had the honor to lead since 1999. Kraków was an essential base for, as well as a subject of, my research on *Witness to Hope: The Biography of Pope John Paul II*. And it was during those years (1996–99) that I came to know the men and women of Karol Wojtyła's *Środowisko*, whom John Paul II had urged me to meet in order to know him "from the inside." Happily, some of John Paul's best friends became close friends of mine, too, and those friendships have been deepened during my annual July visits to the city. Kraków was, once again, my research base as I was preparing the second volume of my John Paul II biography, *The End and the Beginning: Pope John Paul II—The Victory of Freedom, the Last Years, the Legacy*. In the years immediately before and after that book's publication, I've been honored by invitations to address the "Days of John Paul II" academic symposia organized annually by Krakow's major institutions of higher learning. So I now think of Krakow as one of my homes, and I am deeply grateful to its immensely hospitable people for making me feel as if I'm a Cracovian, *honoris causa*.

Carrie Gress came to Kraków as a student in the Tertio Millennio Seminar in 1999 and then returned as the seminar's project manager from 2001 through 2006. It was during those years that she did some initial research for a different kind of guide to the city, so it seemed the obvious thing to invite her to join in this project and provide the historical notes. My son, Stephen, and I had already done *Roman Pilgrimage: The Station Churches* together, and it seemed just as obvious to me that he should be the project photographer; so he came to Kraków during the July 2014 assembly of the Tertio Millennio Seminar and brought the city alive in ways I hadn't previously imagined through his work.

Many friends in Kraków helped in the preparation of this book. Cardinal Stanisław Dziwisz, longtime secretary of Pope John Paul II and archbishop of Kraków since 2005, was a supporter of this project, and his letter of endorsement opened (and kept open) many doors. Cardinal Dziwisz's secretary, Fr. Tomasz Szopa, was unfailingly helpful. Msgr. Dariusz Raś, the rector of the *Mariacki*, and Agata Wolska of the basilica's staff, made Stephen's and my work there possible. Msgr. Zdzisław Sochacki facilitated the photography in Wawel Cathedral. Father Jacek Pietruszka arranged Stephen's and my visit to the Family Home of John Paul II Museum in Wadowice.

Father Raymond J. de Souza, another Tertio Millennio

Seminar alumnus (and now faculty member) first suggested to me the image of Kraków as the "city where the twentieth century happened"—and where the providential answer to that was also given in the revelations of the Divine Mercy to Sister Maria Faustina Kowalska, the first saint of the twenty-first century. Douglas Farrow, Fr. Jonathan Kalisch, OP, Fr. Jarosław Kupczak, OP, Fr. Michał Mitka, OP, Paula Olearnik, Jan Rybicki, Stephen White, Fr. Maciej Zięba, OP, and several of the sisters at the Shrine of Divine Mercy each helped the project in distinctive ways. It's been a privilege to have Gary Jansen as my editor at Image.

Quotations from the *Diary of St. Maria Faustina Kowalska: Divine Mercy in My Soul* (© 1987 Marian Fathers of the Immaculate Conception of the Blessed Virgin Mary) are used with permission.

Piotr and Teresa Malecki have been close friends for almost two decades. Their extraordinary help in July 2014 prompts me to acknowledge that friendship and solidarity with a special mention in the dedication of this book: which, in its own way, is an extension of what began a long time ago in the formation of *Środowisko*—men and women who helped form a saint, St. John Paul II, who took his "beloved Kraków" with him as he changed the world and the Church in a distinctively Cracovian way.

G.W.

Washington, DC
November 1, 2014
The Solemnity of All Saints

Principal Sites